WILKINSON

3/02

# ADVANCES IN
# CRIMINOLOGICAL THEORY

# ADVANCES IN CRIMINOLOGICAL THEORY

## Volume One

*Edited by*

**William S. Laufer**
**and**
**Freda Adler**

Transaction Publishers
New Brunswick (U.S.A.) and Oxford (U.K.)

Second printing, 1995.

Copyright (c) 1989 by Transaction Publishers, New Brunswick, New Jersey 08903.

Library of Congress Catalog Number: 88-4940
ISBN: 0-88738-182-0
Printed in the United States of America

**Library of Congress Cataloging-in-Publication Data**

Advances in criminological theory / edited by William S. Laufer and Freda Adler.
   p. cm.
   Includes index.
   ISBN: 0-88738-182-0
   1. Crime and criminals.  I. Laufer, William S.  II. Adler, Freda.
HV6018.A39 1988
364-dc19
                                          88-4940
                                          CIP

# Contents

To Freda with
the best wishes of
Mortimer Heller

# Preface

*Marvin E. Wolfgang*

Criminology—or, if you wish, criminal justice as well as criminology—has become a separate scientific discipline. The canons of the scientific method form the belief system of this discipline. The methods of science from Aristotle to Bacon, Newton to Comte and Durkheim—to move from physical to social science—involve the building of theory from postulates to hypotheses, testing, analyses, interpretations, including inferences and implications. These are golden terms, often abused, in scientific writing.

What has happened in criminology and criminal justice in the United States since World War II has been a rushing but welcome thrust toward more and more hard-core, quantitatively empirical research that has moved from simple bivariate to multivariate regression models and path, logit, and survival analyses. These have been healthy movements that have put United States criminology in the vanguard of research methodology. European and Asian scholars come to the United States to study and to emulate our efforts to improve the scientificity of the discipline.

What about the development of theory? Criminology, for thirty years at least, has been mostly descriptive and internally analytical, that is, analytical within the confines of the data observed and described. There is nothing wrong with that process, but it has produced no new, fascinatingly provocative (whether wrong or correct) theory. Yes, we have strain and stress theory, social control theory, due process legal theory, social conflict theory, some labeling that never achieved theory status, new radical and critical criminology, and subcultural theory. Nothing so significant has emerged since World War II as Sutherland's differential association or Sellin's culture conflict and crime.

In *Evaluating Criminology* (Elsevier, 1979), I and my colleagues Robert Figlio and Terence Thornberry reviewed the development of methodological and theoretical works, in criminology over twenty-eight years, from 1945 to 1972. The quality of works, as judged by the citation index, peer evaluations, and our own content analysis, did improve slightly. But there was no significant new theoretical development.

There is a new journal concerned with quantitative criminology. My former student James A. Fox launched it as chief editor. I am on the Board of Editors and obviously applaud it. I am now equally pleased to applaud a new serial on theory in criminology, launched by William Laufer and by one of my former students, Freda Adler, who was also a student of Thorsten Sellin's.

There is a need for a theory serial. Our major journals–the *Journal of Criminal Law and Criminology* and *Criminology*–can, of course, entertain theoretical manuscripts. But such manuscripts compete with the chi-squares and logit models of quantitative research, and the "hard" science commonly wins out over the "soft" science. However, let us not demur on that often false dichotomy. The theory this serial intends to publish will be as hard–meaning a logically structured, sound, and sophisticated "grand" or Mertonian "middle-range" theory–as authors can present. Rich heurism is invited, but rhetoric and speculation not rooted in empirical observations, or theory not inductively derived, will receive no notice.

This serial is launched with the intention to encourage innovative thinking from scholars anywhere in the world. Theory in criminology has been stagnant for decades. Criminology has always borrowed theory from sociology, psychology, economics, and other disciplines. Is there a special theory of crime, criminality, and society's response? Let us see. Let us look forward to the seminal submissions from new and young scholars with fresh ideas, and from elder statesmen who can reflect on years of accumulated erudition.

The dedication of this first volume to Thorsten Sellin is a dedication to his relatively youthful contribution in 1938 of *Culture Conflict and Crime*, as well as a dedication to his continued contributions, through his ninetieth birthday, such as the translation of Mark Ancel's book *Social Defense*. With this first volume we hail Thorsten Sellin and all future writings in criminological theory.

# Introduction:
# The Challenges of Advances in
# Criminological Theory

## William S. Laufer and Freda Adler

Over the past several decades there has been a strong movement in criminology to ensure a methodological thoroughness and technical exactness that resembles, in many respects, that which is found in the repertoire of the physical sciences. Few would deny the importance of this trend, given the evolution of the "scientific" study of crime. Unfortunately, though, no parallel movement has been at work to encourage good theory. Moreover, the strong mandate to "do science" has invited a risk that the exchange of ideas or hypotheses—often the building blocks of theory—will be demeaned or stripped of status. Some would argue that this already has happened.

At the very least it is apparent that the current emphasis on matters of design, methods, and data analysis can foster an inhibition of creative intuition. Even a casual reading of our journals is sufficient testimonial to this assertion. Thus, the primary reason for creating *Advances* is to encourage the exchange of ideas in a forum that is both receptive to, and yet appropriately critical of, educated speculation and innovation. Contributions will appear in the form of theoretical deliberations, theory construction, and efforts to test the validity and reliability of extant theories of crime and criminality.

### Four Challenges of Advancing Criminological Theory

It is natural to react with both excitement and skepticism when a new social science periodical is announced. There are already many publications supporting the relatively small interdisciplinary field of criminology. It is therefore entirely fair to question why yet another is needed. The answer is straightforward. *Advances* may be justified in the context of a number of challenges to the field of criminology. It would be impossible to do justice to all of these challenges in this brief introduction, but it is important to note a few of the more potent ones.

*Levels of Analysis*

Historically, it has been acceptable and customary to design and conduct theoretically relevant research with one of two goals in mind: explanation of the existence of crime or criminal behavior. The focus was squarely on the explicandum. Little effort was expended to acknowledge the level of analysis adopted or the appropriateness of the design to the level of analysis offered. For example, criminologists popularized Hirschi's (1969) notion of social control as an explanation of conformity on an individual *and* group level without much concern for the uniqueness of its application or utility to either. Sutherland's theory of differential association has been interpreted in much the same manner (Sutherland and Cressey, 1974).

We have continually disregarded or confused levels of analysis when dismissing the relative strengths of individual explanations of criminality, and likewise are all too often blind to macrolevel theory, when discussing individual-level correlates of behavior. All of this might have been tolerable at a time when the orientations of psychologists and sociologists were easily discernible and their numbers were small. Our field, however, has grown and so, too, has the number of scholars with bidisciplinary training and generalist criminal justice backgrounds, many of whom have an interest in integrative study. In short, it is no longer fruitful to search for explanations without reflecting on the level of analysis employed. Without such reflection there is danger because we risk and often invite confusion. This confusion can take the form of dismissing the importance of a variable such as social class when engaged in a microlevel investigation, or the dismissal of certain personality correlates when involved in a macrolevel study. Both may have explanatory power, but only at a certain level of analysis. Consider, for example, Rodney Stark's (1987) recent revelations surrounding his effort to demonstrate the insulating effect of religious commitment on deviance.

Stark conducted some of the early work on religiosity and delinquency in the late 1960s, and had hoped that his data would demonstrate a negative relation. Despite a large sample, acceptable measures of pertinent variables, and "considerable statistical manipulation," he and his colleagues failed to find a significant effect (Hirschi and Stark, 1969; Stark and Glock, 1968). Stark was not alone in his inability to demonstrate a relation between religion and criminality. It is notable that subsequent efforts were nothing short of equivocal (Stark, 1987). After some time Stark raised the issue once again, and it is now apparent that the problem was not one of original intuition, but rather a matter of failing to consider the level of analysis. As Stark admits,

> I soon discovered that so long as religion is conceived of as an individual trait, as a set of personal beliefs and practices, we can never know when and where religion will influence conformity, for research will continue to produce contradictory findings. But, if we move from a psychological to a sociological conception of religion, clarity leaps from chaos. I am prepared to argue theoretically and to demonstrate empirically that religion affects conformity, not through producing guilt or fear of hellfire in the individual, but that religion gains its power to shape the individual only as an aspect of groups [1987, p. 112].

Stark's experience provides a simple yet powerful illustration of the importance of knowing not only the *explicandum*, or what it is that is being explained (e.g. crime or delinquency) but at what level the explanation is taking place (e.g. individual or group behavior). This simple caveat is not new or novel. Stark's journey might have been far less exhausting if Emile Durkheim had been along. At the turn of the century, Durkheim had wisely derived the following principle and revelation:

> The determining cause of a social fact must be sought among antecedent social facts and not among states of individual consciousness. . . . The function of a social fact must always be sought in its relation to some social end. . . . It is because sociologists have often misunderstood this rule and have considered social phenomena from too psychological a point of view that many of their theories seem too vague, imprecise, and far removed from the specific character of the things they are intended to explain [p. 74].

It seems clear, then, that maintaining an awareness of levels of analysis is important while formulating research questions and deliberating over questions of design and method. It is of particular concern in the conceptualization of integrative and interdisciplinary studies, in which researchers tend to join or merge micro and macro levels of explanation. But perhaps it is most crucial in constructing interventions based upon the theoretical revelations derived from a particular study or series of studies. It is worth wondering about the prognosis for crime control and prevention programs that derive from theoretically rich investigations that neglect consideration of levels of analysis. Therefore, the first challenge posed by *Advances* is to encourage efforts that maintain an awareness of the level of analysis of a theoretical premise, proposition, or study.

### Explanas-Explicandum Congruence

A second challenge is related to the first but is more general. This challenge calls for a heightened awareness of the relation between a theory and what a theory explains. Theories of crime, criminal behavior, deviance, and conformity, for example, are often constructed and validated with a specific and clearly articulated *explicandum*. The general propositions that make up a theory, or that which explains (*Explanas*), should bear a logical and demonstrable relation to the explicandum (Hempel, 1965; Walker, 1975). In other words, a theory of gang delinquency may be inappropriate as an explanation of embezzlement; a crime-specific theory may fail as a general theory of deviance; and a general theory of criminal behavior may be inadequate as explanatory of certain criminal acts. Although this seems quite obvious, too frequently the attraction or allegiance to a particular theoretical orientation seems to result in applications for which there is little justification. Therefore, the second challenge is to attend to the logic of this explicandum-explanas consistency.

*Grand Theory versus Incremental Disciplinary Explanations*

For some, wrestling with criminological theory seems to hold appeal because it forces attention to some of the most revered and ultimate questions in criminology, such as, What causes crime? This understandable attraction has tempted many to derive grand theories that, allegedly, account for all criminal behavior.

One such brand of grand theory is derived from combining a number of often conflicting theories (Elliot, Ageton, and Cantor, 1979). A related but different approach seeks to explain crime or deviance from a collection of selected variables taken from different theoretical perspectives (e.g. Johnson, 1979). A third and final response to temptation has been to suggest a grand theory from within one particular discipline (e.g. psychoanalytic theory has been credited with final "answers" as to why crime occurs) (cf. Hirschi, 1969).

Before commenting on the integrity of these three approaches, it is only fair to air some concerns that have been raised about integrative and interdisciplinary efforts. It can be argued that the fundamental limitation of each of these three grand approaches is their prematurity. Too little appears to be known about each disciplinary perspective, and far too few perspectives are known, for there to be much gained from such global integrations. Interpreting the puzzle of crime becomes that much more difficult when some of the pieces either are absent, incomplete, or in an inexact form. One might argue that this is what we have settled for. If so, then there should be more support for the notion that the body of theoretical literature will benefit most from incremental disciplinary investigations.

More specifically, the first approach, which combines a group of theories in order to explain crime, suffers from the limitations of each theory—as

Hirschi (1969) has noted—and also is limited by the theories not considered. It may be, for example, that personological or situational perspectives would have accounted for far more variance in Elliot's integration than the traditional sociological propositions employed. Does this mean that each and every theory of crime causation must be incorporated into such an integration? Do we know enough about the explanatory power of situational variables to dismiss them in such a global integration? And finally, are we comfortable with the notion that microlevel theory and macrolevel theory can coexist in an integration? Perhaps we should consider their differing level of analysis.

There is a similar problem where criminologists have sought to explain deviance, delinquency, or criminality by selecting preferred variables from a number of different theories. The validity of the integration and the amount of variance that can be explained are actually a product of the investigator's judgment in selecting variables for inclusion in a particular model. This judgment is limited further by what is known or hypothesized about the power of each variable. All too often variables are chosen for reasons that appear arbitrary or artificial: dismissing the power of variables for reasons found in disciplinary bias, or budgetary limitations. An example of the former may be seen in the work of Johnson (1979), who dismisses psychological and biological factors from his model of the origins of juvenile delinquency because they lack empirical support as general explanations.

Finally, there is the infrequent assertion that a singular theory derived from one discipline accounts for all crime. It may be said that the assertion's infrequency is evidence of its soundness. There are many good reasons for criminology's evolution into an interdisciplinary field, however, and its being so illustrates the limitations of such an assertion.

On the other hand, in an effort to increase the sophistication of bivariate or univariate models, some researchers, it seems, are too quick to point out the limitations of such an approach to the study of crime causation. For example, the crime-personality relation has met with some disfavor over the past decade as situationalists have noted person-situation interactions, as well as equivocal evidence for the consistency of personality over time (e.g. Pervin, 1987). Assuming the validity of the situationalist claims—as most do—should these revelations inhibit efforts, for instance, to test the power of personality measures to predict delinquency without considering situations? If there is *any* power in a personological variable, must it be studied in context of the situation to advance our understanding of criminological theory?

Our criticism of these approaches suggests that a renewed focus on increasing the power of our disciplinary explanations of criminality may be indicated, with the long-range goal of perfecting interdisciplinary integration. The next challenge, therefore, is simply to bolster the validity of the pieces in the puzzle while trying to resist inappropriate integrative temptation.

*The Criminology of Criminal Justice*

There are three common replies to the question, Are there any meaningful differences between criminology and criminal justice? First, the traditional response suggests the obvious: the former is an ancient import that has been refined by modern sociology; the latter was born within the last several decades and is a marriage of many disciplines, such as psychology, sociology, biology, law, geography, and education. Beyond these often artificial disciplinary divisions, it is said that criminology generally concerns itself with the scientific study of crime and criminals, and that criminal justice is strictly a systems-based discipline, focused by its very definition on process and justice-related questions.

A second response is that there is no meaningful difference between the two endeavors, or that the differences are more apparent than real. Proponents of this view generally are graduates of an eclectic criminal justice education, who have been trained in a melange of psychology, sociology, biology, and related social sciences, and who have a devotion or commitment to planned change. More than likely, they perceive the criminal justice system as a complex environment requiring scientific study as a basis for any intervention.

A third response is a variant of the second; it acknowledges the differences between criminology and criminal justice but maintains that the latter is founded upon the precepts of the former. Although this contention runs counter to conventional wisdom, it seems most plausible.

Disciplinary partisanship and educational orientation often support an unfortunate notion that theories of crime causation and criminality are the fixtures of tired academicians in university clubs. Some grant-giving foundations and institutions have helped this notion along by frowning at the sight of a theory-laden proposal—why fund such an effort, given its limited or nonexistent applicability? One might fairly conclude that (a) our criminal justice system is atheoretical, (b) the theories that provide a basis for the criminal justice system have been received critically, or (c) theory in its present form has little utility.

Quite obviously, even a superficial exposure to the nature of each successive process in the criminal justice system suggests a reliance on criminological theory, whether born from intuition or derived from empirical study. The most apparent reliance may be seen in programmatic efforts to prevent and control juvenile delinquency, but clearly the system is graced with theory at the time of law enforcement, in deliberations over the granting of bail, as well as at sentencing.

We are left with the unfortunate reality that the popular dichotomy of theory/system or criminology/criminal justice is likely prompted by the inadequacy of extant theory. How inadequate are existing conceptions of crime and criminality? For the purposes of providing a context and justification for system processes and policies, theoreticians have only to reflect on the success rate of most correctional interventions, or prison recidivism rates, to see a few of the many challenges that remain. Thus, the service that criminology may bring to the criminal justice system forms the fourth and final challenge.

## Concluding Thoughts

*Advances* is published at a time of significant growth, as well as a disturbing level of insulation, in criminology. It would be only a slight exaggeration to say that a new and impressive language of criminology has emerged, along with a handful of sophisticated theories that, for a variety of reasons, are familiar only to criminologists. Compounding this "separate" identity are increased numbers of criminal justice scholars and equivalent "generalists" who maintain a fluency solely in the dialect of criminology.

As a result, there is an even greater need now than ever before to remain current with, and well versed in, the advance of allied disciplines. We tend to borrow from them years later, often inattentive to the birth of new trends, innovations, and subtle ideological movements. This is unfortunate because we do have a convenient window through which we can view their work, whether or not they view ours. It is our hope (albeit an ambitious one) that *Advances* will find a cross-disciplinary audience as well as track relevant movements and advances in allied fields.

Finally, few would argue with the idea that the evolution of criminological theory has been determined, or at least molded, by a greater worldview. Whom criminologists study, the behaviors chosen for examination, and the extent to which society is credited with some responsibility in determining the actions of an offender appear to reflect a broad vision of criminology. This vision can easily be blurred by a compelling philosophical allegiance to positivist teachings, or simply by a distaste for the rhetoric that can, and often does, accompany critical, new, or Marxist expositions. For this reason, the editors of *Advances* will maintain an awareness of, and an openness to, the multiple roles that theoreticians of crime can play in defining appropriate objects of study and in constructing resulting explanations.

## References

Durkheim, E. 1981. Methods of Explanation and Analysis. In A. Giddens (ed.) *Emile Durkheim: Selected Writings.* Cambridge: Cambridge University Press.
Elliot, D.S., S.S. Ageton, and R.J. Cantor. 1979. "An Integrated Theoretical Perspective on Delinquent Behavior." *Journal of Research in Crime and Delinquency* 16:327.
Hempel, C.G. 1965. *Aspects of Scientific Explanation and Other Essays in the Philosophy of Science.* New York: Free Press.
Hirschi, T. 1969. *Causes of Delinquency.* Berkeley: University of California Press.
Hirschi, T., and R. Stark. 1969. "Hellfire and Delinquency." *Social Problems* 17:202-13.
Johnson, R.E. 1979. *The Origins of Juvenile Delinquency.* New York: Cambridge University Press.
Stark, R., 1987. "Religion and Deviance: A New Look." In *Crime, Values and Religion*, edited by J.M. Day and W.S. Laufer. Norwood, N.J.: Ablex.
Stark, R. and C.Y. Glock. 1968. *American Piety.* Berkeley: University of California Press.
Sutherland, E.H., and D.R. Cressey. 1974. *Criminology.* 9th ed. Philadelphia: Lippincott.
Walker, N. 1975. *Behavior and Misbehavior.* New York: Basic Books.

# 1

# Criminological Theories: The Truth as Told by Mark Twain

*Don M. Gottfredson*

Theories in criminology tend to be unclear and lacking in justifiable generality. The lack of clarity results in apparent inconsistencies, although more attention to the structure of a scientific theory and its requirements might reveal more agreement among theorists than now recognized. Or, it might reveal sharp disagreements, helping to identify conflicts among theories in such a way that they could be decided by critical tests. Science usually progresses by such competition when the debate can be decided empirically. Now, when an author chooses among theories as may seem suitable to the argument made, it is politely called eclecticism, but its probably true name is incoherence.

Rarely do available theories offer practical guidance that does not require heroic leaps of conjecture. Practicality is not a requisite of a valid theory (a theory might be true yet void of utility), but a good theory may be required for practicality. Kurt Lewin's often quoted remark that "nothing is as practical as a good theory" may be correct, but perhaps it may be said also that nothing is so impractical as a poor one. Now, weak or poorly defined concepts steer major criminal justice policy decisions. This may be due to the same lack of attention to the fundamental requirements associated with the various parts of a theory and its development.

Criminologists should pay increased attention to some fundamental tenets of scientific theory building. These are not new (I have not invented them), and they are accepted widely. Certain critical choices must be made, and they should be made explicitly. The purpose of this paper is to offer a set of concerns that may be useful in evaluation of any theory.

Fortunately, to make my points I need not embarrass either my crimi-

1

nological friends or myself. The nature of scientific theories has long since been described by Mark Twain, an astute philosopher of science, now deceased and hence incapable of complaint.

### Twain: Theoretician and Criminologist

Samuel Langhorne Clemens, alias Mark Twain (among other names used as the occasion seemed to require), claimed to be a humorist. (He also claimed to be a liar, but I cannot support that with citations because the full documentation would use up my allotment for references.) He is especially noted for, besides his place in world literature, his social, art, moral philosophy, and literary criticism, but he was a critic also of the philosophy of science and had an excellent understanding of the scientific method. He liked the method so much that he wished scientists used it more often. (He was also, like most people, a part-time criminologist.) He supported my view of his disguise as a humorist in his autobiography (to be read after his death when he would be "unaware and indifferent") in the following way:

> Humor is only a fragrance, a decoration. . . . There are those who say a novel should be a work of art solely and you must not preach in it, you must not teach in it.

> That may be true as regards novels but it is not true as regards humor. Humor must not professedly teach and it must not professedly preach, but it must do both if it is to live forever. By forever, I mean thirty years. . . . I have always preached. That is the reason I have lasted thirty years. If the humor came of its own accord and uninvited I have allowed it a place in my sermon, but I was not writing the sermon for the sake of the humor. I should have written the sermon just the same, whether any humor applied for admission or not. I am saying these vain things in this frank way because I am a dead person speaking from the grave. Even I would be too modest to say them in life. I think we never become really and genuinely our entire and honest selves until we are dead—and not then until we have been dead years and years. People ought to start dead and then they would be honest so much earlier [no date b:298].

In another example, Twain wrote:

> I have been forced by fate to adopt fiction as a medium of truth. Most liars lie for the love of the lie; I lie for the love of the truth. I dissemble my true views by means of a series of apparently humorous and mendacious stories [1967:8].

## Requirements for a Theory

Theories consist of postulates, theoretical constructs, logically derived hypotheses, and definitions. Theories can be improved steadily through hypothesis testing, examination of evidence from observations, revisions of the theory, and repetitions of the cycle, repeatedly modifying the theory in light of the evidence. Although these theory characteristics seem straightforward, one usually searches in vain for explicit statements of the basic assumptions underlying criminological theories. They may be present, if one can find them hidden here and there throughout the exposition, or they may be merely implicit. Sometimes a careful search for assumptions will turn up conflicting ones [Kornhauser, 1978]. Often it is difficult to tell whether a statement is regarded as a postulate or a hypothesis, or whether it is made on the basis of empirical observation. The theoretical constructs central to the theory may or may not be defined, or they may be used with apparently different meanings throughout the essay. Statements of hypotheses may include terms inadequately defined, or of questionable and untested reliability of measurement, or of an obscure relation to the concepts included in the assumptions—that is, of problematic construct validity. Each of these main parts of the structure of a theory is of utmost importance.

The provision by scientific method for improvement of the theory may not be used to advantage. Tests of hypotheses may be wholly lacking, flawed, or of dubious generalization. Rarely is the theory revised in the light of the evidence.

## Postulates

The proper starting point is a set of postulates. A postulate is an assumption. An assumption is, by definition, not proved but taken on faith, either on the basis of plausibility or because it is believed that it will be fruitful for the theory. An example, basic to all science, which aims at understanding, prediction, and control, is that there is organization in nature. We cannot prove it, but the alternative postulate—that nature is chaotic—hardly could be expected to be productive for the development of scientific theories.

There are other postulates common to science. The postulate of natural kinds asserts that resemblances occur in large numbers and provides the basis for classification, which is fundamental to science. The postulate of permanence, that nature is relatively stable over time, undergirds prediction. Because this postulate has not been thought to be absolutely true since Heraclitus, the word *relatively* is necessary; and it commonly is assumed that although nature changes, change occurs slowly. The postulate of natural determinism is another staple of the scientist. It now must be reconciled with probabilism, unless one is to take Bertrand Russell (a sometime humorist disguised as a philosopher) seriously when he considered that God created the universe as a determinist and then left it all to chance. These and other postulates are common to all science, and it is not to be expected that criminological theorists recite them as they begin their theory building. But criminological theories contain, sometimes explicitly but more often implicitly, a further set of assumptions that should be identified as such. In criminological theory building (as in psychological, sociological, and other social theory construction) it is curious and disconcerting that once the basic assumptions have been identified (even if seemingly hidden), they soon are seen to be taken for fact. Mark Twain, discussing disputes about who Shakespeare really was, was impressed at how a very few facts can generate assumptions that can quickly be transformed into strongly held beliefs, and how, even absent any facts, presumptions may be taken as a starting point for an entire explanatory system, which then is accepted as having a firm empirical basis. Here is how he described that transition:

> The thugs presume it—on no evidence of any kind. Which is their way, when they want a historical fact. Fact and presumption are, for business purposes, all the same to them. They know the difference, but they also know how to blink it. They know, too, that while in history building a fact is better than a presumption, it doesn't take a presumption long to bloom into a fact when *they* have the handling of it. They know by old experience that when they get hold of a presumption-tadpole he is not going to *stay* tadpole in their history tank; no, they know how to develop him into the giant four-legged bull frog of *fact*, and make him sit up on his hams, and puff out his chin, and look important and insolent and come-to-say; and assert his genuine simon-pure authenticity with a thundering bellow that will convince everybody because it is so loud. The thug is aware that loudness convinces sixty persons where reasoning convinces but one [1963 c:442].

Presumptions may be mistaken for facts by both scientists and policymakers when central theoretical concepts either are not recognized as assumed or are not defined in a scientifically acceptable manner. Examples of theoretical assumptions taken as fact abound in criminology: the "social nature of man," the "class-crime relations," the "futility of rehabilitation" are only a few examples.

Twain may have been part natural determinist, occasionally supernatural determinist, part probabilist, part free willer. But it is clear that he accepted the postulate of permanence, though only as modified to allow for change. On consistency in nature (providing also some hints at the probabilistic nature of the universe), Twain reported on a lecture he invented by a Professor of Historical Forecast discussing two laws of one Reginald Selkirk, "commonly called the Mad Philosopher." These were the "Law of Intellectual Averages" and the "Law of Periodical Repetition."

> By the terms of the Law of Periodical Repetition nothing whatever can happen a single time only; everything happens again, and yet again, and still again—monotonously. Nature has no originality—I mean, no large ability in the matter of inventing new things, new ideas, new stage effects. She has a superb and amazing and infinitely varied equipment of old ones, but she never adds to them. She repeats—repeats—repeats. ... When she puts together a man, and is satisfied with him, she is loyal to him, she stands by him through thick and thin forevermore, she repeats him by billions and billions of examples; and physically and mentally the *average* remains exactly the same, it doesn't vary a hair between the first batch, the middle batch and the last batch. If you ask, "But really—do you think all men are alike?" I reply, "I said the *average* does not vary."

> "'But you will have to admit that some individuals do far overtop the average—intellectually, at least.'"

> "'Yes, I answer, and Nature repeats *those*. There is nothing that she doesn't repeat.'"

> "By the Law of Periodical Repetition, everything which has happened once must happen again and again and again—and not capriciously, but at regular periods, and each thing in its own period, not another's, and each obeying its own law.

> ... "Are there any ingenuities whereby you can discredit the law of suicide? No. It is established. If there was such and such a number in such and such a town last year, that number, substantially, will be repeated this year. That number will keep step, arbitrarily with the increase of population, year after year. Given the population a century hence, you can determine the crop of suicides that will be harvested in that distant year."

Yet, part of consistency is change:

> What is the most rigorous law of our being? Growth. No smallest atom of our moral, mental, or physical structure can stand still a year. It grows—it must grow; nothing can prevent it. It must grow downward or upward; it must grow smaller or larger, better or worse—it cannot stand still. In other words, we change—and must change, constantly, and keep on changing as long as we live. What, then, is the true Gospel of consistency? Change. Who is the really consistent man? The man who changes. Since change is the law of his being, he cannot be consistent if he stick in a rut [1963:577].

This paradox, that change is a part of the consistency in nature, was recognized by Twain when he made use of a commonly used, often misused, method of science: linear extrapolation. After describing the shortening of the Mississippi River by cutoffs of horseshoe curves that steadily decreased its length, Twain, suggesting what he would do if he "wanted to be one of those ponderous scientific people," extrapolated in both directions and wrote:

> In the space of one hundred and seventy-six years the Lower Mississippi has shortened itself two hundred and forty-two miles. That is an average of a trifle over one mile and a third per year. Therefore, any calm person, who is not blind or idiotic, can see that in the old Oolitic Silurian Period, just a million years ago next November, the Lower Mississippi was upwards of one million three hundred thousand miles long, and stuck out over the Gulf of Mexico like a fishing rod. And by the same token any person can see that seven hundred and forty-two years from now the Lower Mississippi will be only a mile and three quarters long, and Cairo and New Orleans will have joined their streets together, and will be plodding comfortably along under a single mayor and a mutual board of aldermen. There is something fascinating about science. One gets such wholesale returns of conjecture out of such a trifling investment of fact [1961 a:120].

The projection of prison populations (and hence the need for prisons) today often follows a similar method. The returns to the prison construction industry are substantial.

Beginning with postulates, much of science is deductive, yet its firm basis must be in that which is observed and hence inductive. The danger is in the harvest that may be reaped from "a trifling investment of fact."

Twain's "brief lectures on science" provide a further illustration of the hazards of induction. He shows how, in solving a murder case, "any cultivated paleontologist" could easily substitute, with profit, for a dozen New York detectives. By using nothing but one of the meager clues at the scene of the crime, such a scientist could have

> walked right off and fetched you that murderer with an unerring certainty as he would take a fragment of an unknown bone and build you the animal it used to belong to, and tell you which end its tail was on and what he preferred for dinner. (That, he said, is what "science" can do) [1977:130].

The ease with which modern criminological theory can "explain," after the fact, any fragment of the crime problem with the same unerring certainty is another example of what "science" can do.

There are other postulates of science that normally are accepted, as they must be, even though they are demonstrably false or at least suspect. This is one reason that the theorist must maintain the healthy skepticism that is the hallmark of the scientific orientation. For three examples, consider that science relies on the objectivity of perception, the logic of reasoning, and the accuracy of memory. Each is demonstrably unreliable to some degree, yet all knowledge is based upon them.

As to perception, it is well recognized by scientists that it is necessary to seek the avoidance of bias in observation. Careful reasoning, besides its obvious need for development of a coherent theory, requires the avoidance of overgeneralization from biased samples. Twain's critique of a description of Americans by a visitor from France is instructive. When Paul Bourget visited the United States and went home to France to tell about it, Twain examined his method:

> I saw by his own intimations that he was an Observer and had a System—that used by naturalists and other scientists. The naturalist collects many bugs and reptiles and butterflies and studies their ways a long time patiently. By this means he is presently able to group these creatures into families and subdivisions of families by nice shadings of differences observable in their characters. Then he labels all those shaded bugs and things with nicely descriptive group names, and is now happy, for his great work is completed, and as a result he intimately knows every bug and shade of bug there, inside and out. It may be true, but a person who was not a naturalist would feel safer about it if he had the opinion of the bug. I think it is a pleasant System, but subject to error.
>
> The Observer of Peoples has to be a Classifier, a Deducer, a Generalizer, a Psychologizer; and, first and last, a Thinker. He has to be all of these, and when he is at home, observing his own folk, he is often able to prove competency. But history has shown that when he is abroad observing unfamiliar peoples the chances are heavily against him. He is then a naturalist observing a bug, with no more than a naturalist's chance of being able to tell the bug anything new about itself, and no more than a naturalist's chance of being able to teach it any new ways which it will prefer to its own [1897:182-3].

Twain had much to say on the subject of generalization from biased samples. Advocating that the only observer of real value was what he termed the "native novelist," one who had lived among the people and absorbed their manners, speech, character, and ways of life for twenty-five years, he wrote:

> Does the native novelist try to generalize the nation? No, he lays plainly before you the ways and speech and life of a few people grouped in a certain place—his own place—and that is one book. In time he and his brethren will report to you the life and the people of the whole nation—the life of a group in a New England village; in a Texas village; in an Oregon village; in villages in fifty States and Territories; then the farm-life in fifty States and Territories; a hundred patches of life and groups of people in a dozen widely separated cities. And the Indians will be attended to; and the cowboys; and the gold and silver miners; and the Negroes; and the Idiots and Congressmen; and the Irish, the Germans, the Italians, the Swedes, the French, the Chinamen, the

> Greasers; and the Catholics, the Methodists, the Presbyterians; the Congregationalists, the Baptists, the Spiritualists, the Mormons, the Shakers, the Quakers, the Jews, the Campbellites, the infidels, the Christian Scientists, the Mind-Curists, the Faith-Curists, the train robbers, the White Caps, the Moonshiners. And when a thousand able novels have been written, *there* you have the soul of the people, the life of the people, the speech of the people; and not anywhere else can these be had. And the shadings of character, manners, feelings, ambitions, will be infinite [1897:190].

Further relevant to the assumption of logical reasoning, Twain continued to emphasize his thesis about unwarranted generalizations, ridiculing Bourget's description of "the nature of the people" of the United States of America:

> There isn't a single human characteristic that can be safely labelled "American." There isn't a single human ambition, or religious trend, or drift of thought, or peculiarity of education, or code of principles, or breed of folly, or style of conversation, or preference for a particular subject for discussion, or form of legs or trunk or head or face or expression or complexion, or gait, or dress, or manners, or disposition, or any other human detail, inside or outside, that can rationally be generalized as "American" [1897:190].

Similarly, there is no single human characteristic that can safely be labeled "criminal." The word *criminal*, as used in everyday language, does not describe any state of a person in the way that any reliable diagnostic category would. In common usage, it does not refer to any nosological category with any evidence of demonstrable reliability or validity. The word commonly refers to a combination of personal behavior and events as defined by the criminal law and by various actors in the criminal justice system, that is, the behavior of others. In criminological theory building, there is much clarity to be gained by recognition that the word, when used carelessly, may reflect either person characteristics or a person's status with respect to the criminal justice system, or both. Thus, it may be very useful, as discussed by Michael Gottfredson and Travis Hirschi in this volume, to distinguish carefully between propensities toward doing crimes (person characteristics) and crime events (Gottfredson and Hirschi, 1987).

That memory plays tricks on us is well known also, a phenomenon often overlooked in tests of criminological theories.

> In 1847 we were living in a large white house on the corner of Hill and Main Streets—a house that still stands but isn't large now although it hasn't lost a plank: I saw it a year ago [written in 1903] and noticed that shrinkage [Twain, no date b:59].

In self-report studies of delinquent and criminal behavior, in retrospective case-history taking, in other testimony, potential bias in reporting from memory often is overlooked. (A more careful attention in victim surveys has provided a notable exception.)

## Theoretical Constructs

Once it is known what the theory builder postulates, it is normally the case that some concepts will have been invented that require definition. Examples that come to mind might be such terms as *anomie, superego, neutralization, differential association, opportunity, id, self-esteem, delinquency, career criminal, bonding, control, needs, wants, learning, social learning, self-control, ego control, social control, socialization, prisonization, attachment, strain, alienation, reinforcement, punishment,* and so on, but I shall not use them for the reason already explained. Please note that I am not arguing that these may not be useful concepts, but only that the matter of how they are defined is of great importance. I will use an example from Twain's criminological works.

Thoroughly content in his study one day in 1876, Twain was surprised to see a "shriveled, shabby dwarf" enter, every feature a trifle out of shape, yet bearing a "remote and ill-defined resemblance" to the author himself. Even the behavior of the little manikin seemed a disconcerting caricature of Twain. After much berating of the author for his (acknowledged) flaws of behavior, about which the little creature was intimately informed, it was revealed that the deformed little man was his *conscience*, ordinarily an invisible spirit but suddenly made visible to the author alone. The report contains much valuable information about consciences; how they differ among persons, grow, and shrink, for example. Twain's was shrunken and deformed from abuse and neglect. Due to one fortuitous instance, Twain was at last able to leap up, grab his conscience, and, as long desired in fantasy, tear him to shreds, reporting that at last and forever he was a free man. His conscience was dead. He described the next result:

> I settled all my outstanding scores, and began the world anew. I killed thirty-eight persons during the first two weeks—all of them on account of ancient grudges. I burned a dwelling that interrupted my view. I swindled a widow and some orphans out of their last cow, which is a very good one, though not a thoroughbred, I believe. I have also committed scores of crimes, of various kinds, and have enjoyed my work exceedingly, whereas it formerly would have broken my heart and turned my hair gray, I have no doubt [Twain, 1961 b:301].

The main theoretical construct in this criminological theory is the conscience. It is intuitively plausible, used in our everyday conversation, similar in conceptualization to one in perhaps the most influential theory of personality development of recent history, psychoanalysis, and shows up often in discussion of psychopathy or sociopathy (the distinction, if any, being, like the concepts themselves, rather unclear). But what kind of construct is it? It is a spirit, a homunculus, usually but not always invisible. Is it a hypothetical construct? An intervening variable? These are the two types of theoretical constructs most often used and most useful to a careful theory builder. Usually, like Twain, the theorist does not reveal which is intended. Often these constructs are used unconventionally, and often they have acquired what Reichenbach (1951) termed "surplus meaning" and consequently add ambiguity rather than clarity.

Such constructs are extremely important because they tie together the postulates of a theory, its hypotheses, and its empirical propositions. Loose symbolic constructs such as "conscience" may indeed be useful in early stages of the pursuit of understanding; but they do tend to acquire surplus meaning. As stated by Marx (1951:9).

> *Operational validity*, or the open and clearly stated relationship of the construct to its empirical basis in operations producing the data, is the most essential characteristic of construct-formation. Animalistic concepts and others . . . (with surplus meanings) . . . may be tolerated in the early, prescientific development of a field but their replacement by constructs more closely and necessarily tied to the data must occur for scientific advance.

I have asserted that intervening variables and hypothetical constructs are the types of theoretical constructs most apt to be useful in criminological theory building. These have been distinguished and defined in a careful, classic article by MacCorquodale and Meehl (1948). They proposed that the phrase *intervening variable* be restricted to its original meaning as implied by the definition by Tolman (1936), its inventor. As I understand Tolman's intent, an intervening variable is defined (and has meaning only) by its insertion in a functional relation between independent and dependent variables; its meaning is given by an observed empirical relation and nothing else. He explained that psychology is interested in the "to-be-expected behavior of organisms" and

> these predictions, mental processes, . . . will figure only in the guise of objectively definable *intervening variables*. Or, (to borrow a phrase from William James) the sole "cash value" of mental processes lies, I shall assert, in this their character as a set of intermediating functional, processes which interconnect between the initiating causes of behavior, on the one hand, and the final resulting behavior itself, on the other [p. 88].

The clarity and advantage for theory given by intervening variables when they are defined by demonstrable functional relations is apparent from MacCorquodale and Meehl's discussion:

> Such a variable then will be simply a quantity obtained by a specified manipulation of the values of empirical variables; it will involve no hypothesis as to the existence of nonobserved entities or the occurrence of unobserved processes; it will contain, in its complete statement for all purposes of theory and prediction, no words which are not definable either explicitly or by reduction sentences in terms of the empirical variables; and the validity of empirical laws involving only observables will constitute both the necessary and sufficient conditions for the validity of the laws involving these intervening variables [1948:105].

They proposed that the term *hypothetical construct*

> be used to designate theoretical concepts which do *not* meet the requirements for intervening variables in the strict sense [but] . . . involve terms which are not wholly reducible to empirical terms; they refer to processes or entities that are not directly observed (although they need not be in principle unobservable); the mathematical expression of them cannot be formed simply by a suitable grouping of terms in a direct empirical equation; and the truth of the empirical law is a necessary but not a sufficient condition for the truth of these conceptions [1948:106].

In criminological theories, as well as other psychological or sociological ones, what may begin as an intervening variable often becomes transformed, much in the manner of Twain's presumption-tadpole to frog of fact, into hypothetical constructs. Thus, Twain may have introduced the concept "conscience" as though it were an explanatory concept intervening between independent variables of heredity, past experience, or situations and the dependent variable of doing crime, that is, as though it were an intervening variable defined by observable functional relations. If so, he transformed it quickly into a hypothetical construct instead. As illustrated by MacCorquodale and Meehl (1948), the concept of libido (or censor or super-ego) may have been introduced initially in this way, but we find later that

> the libido has acquired certain hydraulic properties, or, as in Freud's former view, that the "energy" of libido has been converted into "anxiety". What began as a name for an intervening variable is finally a name for a "something" which has a host of causal properties. . . . Subsequently we find that certain puzzling phenomena are *deduced* (explained) by means of the various properties of libido, e.g., that it flows, is dammed up, is converted into something else, tends to regress to earlier channels, adheres to things . . . [pp. 108-9].

## Hypotheses

Once the postulates of a theory are clear, and it is clear also what is intended to be the proper role of included theoretical constructs, it remains to logically derive hypotheses. These are theoretical propositions capable of being tested empirically. This requires that the theorist define the variables included in operational terms.

The word *operational* is meant in the sense described by Bridgman (1928). The meaning of a concept is given by the set of operations employed in arriving at the concept. The concept and the operations are synonymous.

Referring to what came to be known as "operationism" and to his astonishment at finding philosophers and scientists not only in agreement but advocating a common method, Stevens wrote about a common assertion in the philosophy of science that

> science seeks to generate confirmable hypotheses by fitting a formal system of symbols (language, mathematics, logic) to empirical observations, and that the propositions of science have empirical significance only when their truth can be demonstrated by a set of concrete operations [1939:].

The testing of hypotheses is, of course, the subject of many books. It is necessary to point out, however, that it is the empirical testing of hypotheses that enables the confirmation or disconfirmation of the theory, can provide for its improvement, and can help distinguish fact from mere conjecture or opinion. One is not entitled to believe in a theory until the evidence is sufficiently convincing.

Twain described the village where Joan of Arc spent her childhood. Near the village was a great oak forest. In it was a dragon:

> It was as long as a tree, and had a body as big around as a tierce, and scales like overlapping great tiles, and deep ruby eyes as large as a cavalier's hat, and an anchor-fluke on its tail as big as I don't know what, but very big, even unusually so for a dragon, as everybody said who knew about dragons. It was thought that this dragon was of a brilliant blue color, with gold mottlings, but no one had ever seen it, therefore this was not known to be so, it was only an opinion. It was not my opinion: I think there is no sense in forming an opinion when there is no evidence to form it on. If you build a person without any bones in him, he may look fair enough to the eye, but he would be limber and cannot stand up; and I consider that *evidence* is the bones of an opinion [no date a:4-5].

Much public policy, in criminal justice as in other fields, is determined not by theories supported by evidence but by opinions lacking bones.

Often the opinions are those of the policymaker and are devoid of any bones whatever, perhaps reflecting imagined public opinion. Others are influenced by measures of public opinion, but even then the bones may be weak, decalcified, arthritic, or bent out of shape:

> Half our people believe in high tariff, the other half believe otherwise. Does this mean study and examination, or only feeling? The latter, I think. I have deeply studied the question, too—and didn't arrive. We all do no end of feeling, and we mistake it for thinking. And out of it we get an aggregation which we consider a boon. Its name is Public Opinion. It is held in reverence. It settles everything. Some think it is the voice of God [1963 b].

After careful study and measurement of opinions related to correctional reform efforts in Maryland in the late 1970s and early 1980s, Stephen Gottfredson and Ralph Taylor observed, *inter alia,*

> Those concerned with correctional reform must have a more sophisticated understanding of the general public than they appear to have had in Maryland. Contrary to popularly accepted opinion, we found the general public to be very supportive of precisely the change strategies which the state was unable to implement. The question of "what the public wants us to do" is paramount—and without good information, based probably on a periodic assessment, we are likely to remain in the grip of "pluralistic ignorance" [1983].

### Reliability and Validity

When the requirements of an adequate theory mentioned so far have been met, it remains also to attend to the concepts of reliability and validity. It is no good to define the concept of a hypothesis in operational terms if its measurement is not reasonably consistent among different observers; and it is useless to the further development of the theory if the concept as defined in that hypothesis does not capture adequately the intent of the theorist in formulating the postulate. As mentioned above, the concept of classification is basic to criminology, as to all science; the next requirement therefore must be to demand the evidence of reliability and validity.

When Fowler was a leading phrenologist of the day, Twain visited him in London, using a fictitious name. After an indifferent fingering of his skull, Twain "came out safe and sound at the end, with a hundred great and shining qualities; but which lost their value and amounted to nothing because each of the hundred was coupled up with an opposing defect which took the effectiveness all out of it." Fowler became "almost interested," however, when he found a *cavity* where a bump should have been and he pronounced that this represented the total absence of the sense of humor. "Hurt, humiliated, and resentful," Twain waited three months until confident that Fowler should have forgotten his face, then went to him again—this time under his own name. Now "the cavity was gone, and in its place was a Mount Everest—figuratively speaking—31,000 feet high, the loftiest bump of humor he had ever encountered in his lifelong experience!"

Later, a friend made a photograph of Twain's right hand and sent it to twelve palmists, concealing Twain's name and asking for estimates of the character of the hand's owner. Included in what Twain considered to be a set of quite undistinguished estimates was one outstanding feature: humor was mentioned only once, and "in that one the palmist said that the possessor of the hand was totally destitute of the sense of humor."

Still later, the experiment was repeated. Two prints of Twain's hands were sent to six distinguished New York City palmists, with his name withheld. "The word humor occurred only once in the six estimates and then it was accompanied by the definite remark that the possessor of the hands was destitute of the sense of humor."

Twain concluded:

> Now then, I have Fowler's estimate, I have the estimates of Stead's six or seven palmists; I have the estimates of Harvey's half-dozen: the evidence that I do not possess the sense of humor is overwhelming, satisfying, convincing, incontrovertible—and at last I believe it myself [note dated b:72-73].

In this instance, of course, Twain failed to distinguish the concepts of reliability and validity—unless he was a humorist.

Classifications of persons and of events are central components of most criminological theories. Rarely are the reliabilities of the classifications reported. Predictive classifications also often occupy fundamental positions in the theories, whether these seek to explain individual or group criminal propensities or crime events. Yet, many studies that even include the word *prediction* in the title report no evidence of the validity of the "predictive" classifications.

### Characteristics of an Adequate Theory

The essentials of an acceptable theory of criminology that may be listed simply on the basis of these considerations are as follows:

1. The basic metasystem, including the theory of knowledge adopted by the theorist, should be clear. This portion of theory construction should include explicit statements of the postulates that form the starting point for the development of the theory.

2. The types of theoretical constructs to be included in the theory should be explained and justified in relation to their empirical meanings.
3. The derivation of hypotheses from the assumptions should be demonstrated to have been done according to accepted rules of logic.
4. Operational definitions of terms used in the hypotheses should be provided, the construct validity of resulting variables should be justified, and evidence of reliabilities should be offered.
5. The empirical evidence bearing on the hypotheses should be presented. Limits to generalizability, both on the basis of definitional concepts of measured variables and on the basis of such considerations as samples observed should be explained.
6. The theory should be reexamined in light of the evidence and revised if necessary.

Absent such adequate theories, one may ponder whether the words of William James, writing about the psychology of the day (1888) may be apt to criminology a century later:

> Whose theories in Psychology have any definitive value today? No one's! Their only use is to sharpen further reflection and observation. The man who throws out the most new ideas and immediately seeks to subject them to experimental control is the most useful Psychologist in the present state of the science [James, 1954:8].

Unless criminological theorists and policymakers pay more strict attention to the logical structure of theory in science, they will continue to educate or reform us in ways we may have trouble understanding or may not want, and we will be in Huckleberry Finn's position at the end of his adventures:

> I reckon I got to light out for the territory ahead of the rest, cause Aunt Sally she's going to adopt me and sivilize me, and I can't stand it. I been there before [Twain, 1960:374].

## References

Bridgman, P.W. 1928. *The Logic of Modern Physics.* New York: Macmillan.
Gottfredson, Michael, and Travis Hirschi. 1987. "A Propensity-Event Theory of Crime." In *Advances in Criminological Theory* 1, edited by W.S. Laufer and F. Adler.
Gottfredson, Stephen, and Ralph B. Taylor. 1983. *The Correctional Crisis: Prison Populations and Public Policy.* Washington, D.C.: Department of Justice, National Institute of Justice, June.

James, William. 1954. Letter to Hugo Munsterberg, as quoted in M. Knight, *William James* (London: Penguin Books, Whitefriars Press).

Kornhauser, Ruth. 1978. *Social Sources of Delinquency.* Chicago: University of Chicago Press.

MacCorquodale, Kenneth, and P.E. Meehl. 1948. "On a Distinction between Hypothetical Constructs and Intervening Variables." *Psychological Review* 55: 95-107.

Marx, M.H., ed. 1951. *Psychological Theory.* New York: Macmillan.

Reichenbach, Hans 1951. *Experience and Prediction,* cited in "The General Nature of Theory Construction," by Melvin H. Marx, in *Psychological Theory,* edited by M.H. Marx. New York: Macmillan.

Stevens, S.S. 1939 "Philosophy and the Science of Science." *Psychological Bulletin* 36: 221-63. See also Stevens's discussions in the same article of what operationism is *not,* and of its relations to logical positivism and the views of the "Vienna Circle."

Tolman, Edward C. 1936. "Operational Behaviorism and Current Trends in Psychology." In *Proceedings of the 25th Celebration of the Inauguration of Graduate Studies.* Los Angeles: University of Southern California Press. Portions reprinted as "The Intervening Variable," in M.H. Marx, ed., *Psychological Theory* (New York: Macmillan, 1951).

Twain, Mark. No date a. *Personal Recollections of Joan of Arc, by The Sieur Louis Conte (her page and secretary), Freely Translated out of the Ancient French into Modern English from the Original Unpublished Manuscript in the National Archives of France by Jean Francois Alden.* New York: Nelson Doubleday.

_____. No date b. *The Autobiography of Mark Twain.* New York: Harper & Row. Originally published by Harper and Brothers in 1959.

_____. 1897. "What Paul Bourget Thinks of Us." In *How To Tell A Story and Other Essays,* pp. 182-83. New York: Harper & Brothers.

_____. 1960. *The Adventures of Huckleberry Finn.* New York: Pocket Books. Copyrighted 1918 by the Mark Twain Company.

_____. 1961 a. *Life on the Mississippi.* New York: Signet Classics.

_____. 1961 b. "The Facts Concerning the Recent Carnival of Crime in Connecticut." In *The Complete Humorous Sketches and Tales of Mark Twain,* edited by C. Neider. Garden City, N.Y.: Doubleday.

_____. 1962. "Passage from a Lecture," in "Papers of the Adams Family." In *Letters from the Earth,* edited by B. De Voto. New York: Harper & Row.

_____. 1963 a. "Consistency" (Paper read at the Hartford Monday Evening Club following the Blaine-Cleveland campaign, 1884). In *The Complete Essays of Mark Twain,* edited by C. Neider. New York: Doubleday.

_____. 1963 b. "Corn-pone Opinions." In *The Complete Essays of Mark Twain,* edited by C. Neider. New York: Doubleday.

_____. 1963 c. "Is Shakespeare Dead?" In *The Complete Essays of Mark Twain,* edited by C. Neider, p. 442. Garden City, N.Y.: Doubleday. Originally published by the Mark Twain Company, 1909.

_____. 1967. Interview published in the Jacksonville, Florida, *Times Union and Citizen,* October 18, 1900, as cited in Sydney J. Krause, *Mark Twain as Critic* (Baltimore: Johns Hopkins University Press), p. 8.

_____. 1977. "A Brace of Brief Lecturers on Science." In *Life as I Find It,* edited by C. Neider, pp. 130-39. New York: Harper & Row.

# 2

# Notes on Criminology and Terrorism

*Austin T. Turk*

Conservative, liberal, and radical perspectives in criminology have been variously described and dissected (e.g. Miller, 1974; Gibbons and Garabedian, 1974; Gibbons, 1979; Inciardi, 1980; Currie, 1985; Vold and Bernard, 1986). The writings and sayings of proponents and critics as well as scholarly commentators indicate at least the commonly accepted reality of this trichotomous sorting of our diverse ways of thinking about things criminal. Most of us, of course, have found it difficult to locate our own views precisely within any one of the three modes as characterized in any particular effort. Accordingly, no one should be offended by the following attempt (1) to describe how the modal conservative, liberal, and radical criminologist, respectively, sees, explains, and would deal with terrorism, or might be expected to do so if interested enough; (2) to note the shortcomings of each in dealing with the realities of terrorism; and (3) to suggest a more promising hybrid approach that incorporates some conservative, liberal, and radical elements.

### Terrorism from Three Perspectives

Even though some criminological notions may be found in, or inferred from, the terrorism literature, the systematic application and development of criminological theory has not been a salient concern. At the same time terrorism has been virtually ignored in criminological theorizing. Consequently, applying the three basic perspectives to terrorism is a largely hypothetical exercise, i.e. extrapolating from what have generally been considered distinctive features of the conservative, liberal, and radical perspectives.

*A Conservative Perspective*

One persistent element in conservative thinking about crime causation is the inclination to presume and search for psychopathology or character defects. Attention to environmental factors tends to be limited to "abnormal" socialization and "alien" cultural traits. Punitive control measures are emphasized, along with efforts to "restore" and defend traditional values, such as familism, localism, stability, and deference to proper authority.

From such a perspective, *terrorism* is an analytically fuzzy and essentially pejorative term for violent incidents attributed to disapproved (especially "leftist" or "communist") political actors and entities. Terrorists are assumed to be defective, warped people whose attacks and threats are nonrational or simply monstrous. Acts against established order (in approved places) are seen as "senseless violence," and the concept of terrorism is generally used only in reference to small-scale ("subrevolutionary") violence in opposition to (approved) state authority.

Attempts to justify terror on tactical, moral, or philosophical grounds are discounted as merely symptomatic or hypocritical. Empirical sources of terrorist thinking and behavior are to be found not so much in observable social inequalities as in the alien ideologies and machinations of foreign adversaries. The possibility that terrorism is indigenous, a product of "our" collective shortcomings, is minimized in favor of a strong presumption that defective characters have been somehow exposed to imported dangerous and irrelevant ("unrealistic") ideas. In short, terrorists are the witting or unwitting carriers of foreign ideological germs—at best misguided defectives, at worst traitorous subversives.

Policies for controlling and preventing terrorism feature repression and xenophobia. Control is to be accomplished by expanding surveillance and other police powers and by improving "counterterrorist" capabilities. Less emphasized than deterrence and incapacitation, prevention measures would include (a) stricter control of immigration and foreign contact, and (b) promoting traditional ethico-religious standards (morality) and political ideals (patriotism). Censorship of objectionable materials and restrictions upon educators, journalists, and other communicators are implied.

*A Liberal Perspective*

Liberal criminology typically assumes and looks for remediable ("middle-range") environmental defects. The guiding postulate is that people behave badly because their past or present circumstances have given them no better options. Constraints upon opportunities to learn and enjoy life's goods (nonmaterial as well as material) have to be identified and removed.

Judicious balancing of collective and individual interests may necessitate coercion on occasion, but emphasis is given to rehabilitation and to prevention through social reforms that minimize inequalities of opportunity. Experienced freedom to develop and express one's individuality presumably makes "antisocial" behavior both an unnecessary and unattractive option.

Such a liberal view of terrorism presumes it to be a particularly ineffective and counterproductive kind of criminal activity. Despite some concern with governmental repression and allusions to "terrorism from above," liberals are inclined to focus upon oppositional terrorism and to treat it as essentially just another form of "criminal violence." Terrorists are assumed to be unfortunate victims of materially and/or culturally inadequate environments, albeit dangerous victims who must be apprehended and rehabilitated.

The "philosophy of the bomb" and related justifications for terror are rejected as products of mistaken beliefs and illogical thinking. However, a distinction is to be made between terrorist acts in "democratic societies" and in "totalitarian societies." In the first, such violence is an unjustifiable but perhaps understandable manifestation of at least "relative deprivation" and/or political frustration. In the second, terrorist violence is both understandable and philosophically justifiable, even though politically simplistic and presumptively counterproductive or at best ineffectual.

Terrorism is to be controlled through law, prevented through education and social reforms. Having originated in movements to assert "the rule of law," liberalism predisposes policymakers to a legalistic approach to terrorism. Established principles of criminal law and procedure are to be applied through "emergency" and special "terrorism" legislation, which formally prohibits specified acts, authorizes certain discretionary practices in apprehending and detaining suspected terrorists, and presumes that accused persons will ultimately be tried and sentenced in accord with accepted procedural rules. Reflecting at least equal concern with prevention, liberal policies aim to promote "mutual tolerance" ("understanding," "people-to-people" contacts, negotiation of differences, education in democratic values) and to improve "opportunity structures" (job creation, expanded welfare supports, socioeconomic development, fostering democratic political institutions). Implicit in such policies is the assumption that "progress" will be orderly and gradual.

## A Radical Perspective

Radical theorizing about crime is characterized by the search for "instrumental" (class, elite) or "structural" (systemic political-economic) villains.

In instrumental thinking, lower-status "conventional" crimes are the products of deprivations imposed by cruel oppressors; "white-collar" or "corporate" crime is essentially a legalistic fiction designed to promote the illusion of impartial justice. In structural thinking, both "street" and "suite" crimes are blamed upon the brutalizing impact of a disapproved (especially "capitalist") social environment. Rather than being defective in some remediable aspects, the environment as a whole is judged to be fundamentally defective. The instrumental solution is to overthrow the oppressors; the structural solution is to destroy the oppressive system—which in practice amounts to the same thing: political revolution.

A radical perspective implies a sharp distinction between governmental and oppositional terrorism, as well as between approved and disapproved political violence. Violence by or on behalf of disapproved regimes, movements, or systems ("capitalist," "reactionary") is "real" terrorism. Such terrorists are monstrous agents of repression and exploitation whose brutality is attributable to sociopathic cruelty and avarice. Terrorist acts by or for approved ("progressive," "anti-kapitalist") causes are to be understood as political behavior, only incidentally, legalistically, or not really criminal. The "good terrorist" is a noble warrior, even though perhaps misguided into "adventurism" by erroneous analysis. "Progressive" terrorist acts demonstrate commitment, and contribute to the revolutionary overthrow of iniquitous regimes and systems.

Efforts to justify disapproved terror are dismissed as ideological mystifications of repression on behalf of exploitation. Justifying approved terror is a matter of understanding that "no one is really innocent" and "all are expendable for the cause," and of recognizing that terror is at times a regrettably necessary tactic within a larger strategy for bringing about revolutionary social changes.

From such a radical perspective, the response to terrorism depends upon whether it is approved or disapproved. Disapproved governmental or subgovernmental "terror from above" is to be met by revolutionary resistance (including "terror from below"). Terrorist opposition to approved regimes or causes is to be crushed without legalistic obstructionism. Preventing terrorism requires macrostructural programs: establishing a total institutional environment designed to maximize collective (not individualized) freedom, i.e. *social* justice. The basic policy issue is whether this is to be achieved through centralization (Leninism, bureaucratization) or decentralization ("participatory democracy," "the mass line").

## A Critical Assessment

Although specialists vary greatly in their conceptions and explanations of terrorism, there is widespread agreement on some aspects:

1. Terrorism is organized political violence.
2. Publicity for "the cause" and intimidation of "third parties" are objectives.
3. Justifications of terror may include factual as well as fanciful, analytical as well as polemical elements.
4. Terrorists are political actors, irrespective of the realism or rationality of their actions.
5. The incidence, prevalence, and forms of terrorist actions are not random but vary with the social dynamics of political, economic, and cultural relationships.
6. Terrorist incidents can be effectively minimized by ruthless repression.
7. Both positive and negative control measures are needed to prevent terrorism.

(For relevant literature reviews, see Laqueur, 1977; Gurr, 1980; *Annals*, 1982; Wardlaw, 1982; Crenshaw, 1983; Freedman and Alexander, 1983; Kerstetter, 1983; Schmid, 1983; Turk, 1982, 1983; Zimmerman, 1983; Han, 1984.) These are, then, the currently understood realities against which conservative, liberal, and radical criminological perspectives on terrorism are to be evaluated.

*Terrorism as Organized Political Violence*

To recognize that terrorism is organized and orchestrated political violence is to accept that violence may be an option and resource for collective action. This implies that terrorist violence is not intrinsically symptomatic of individual pathology but may be a considered political option. Political terror is clearly something other than ordinary criminal violence, and cannot simply be assumed to be ineffective or counterproductive—any more than can other forms of political action (including police and military tactics). One may, of course, approve or disapprove of violence either in general or in specific circumstances, on either ideological (ethical, polemical) or theoretical (analytical, tactical) grounds. But in any case, one cannot begin to understand terrorism without accepting it as a political and collective phenomenon.

Among the three perspectives, the radical is the most sensitive to the politicality and multidimensionality of terrorism; the conservative, the least sensitive; and the liberal, the most ambiguous. The radical perspective rightly encourages understanding that terror is a tactical instrument of political struggle and that it may be used for or against any political interest. At the same time radical thinking tends to exaggerate the political significance and efficacy of approved terror and to play down the meaningfulness of disapproved terror. Conservatives are led to overemphasize the threat of disapproved terror while de-emphasizing or overlooking the dangers of approved terror. In either case their image of disapproved terrorism as merely symptomatic of individual defects is a most inadequate starting point. Liberal understanding of terrorism is confused by the tendency to view it more in narrowly "criminological" than in political terms, and to assume that any violence is unrealistic. In addition, liberals tend to portray terrorism more as aberrant than as systemic, i.e. to neglect political processes in searching for environmental sources of terrorist violence. On balance, the radical perspective is the most promising for developing an adequate conception of terrorism as politically meaningful.

*Objectives of Terrorism*

Terror tactics are adopted because they are expected to be most efficacious for forcing attention to views that negate unacceptable assumptions about what is real and possible, and for intimidating present and potential adversaries. More or less randomized targeting of human and nonhuman objects is virtually the defining characteristic of terrorist violence, for encouraging the fear of unpredictable danger is assumed to be an especially potent way to undermine active and passive support for an opposition. Whatever may be one's ethical views about endangering or using randomly selected victims to attract and influence some audience, the efficacy of terrorist violence remains to be investigated, and decisions regarding its use have to be made.

A liberal antiviolence perspective would seem least conducive to objective consideration of terrorism as either a research subject or a policy option. Conservative thought leaves open the possibility of studying disapproved terrorism (albeit with inadequate conceptual tools), as well as the possible consideration of terror as a political tactic (especially if it is not defined as "terrorism"). From the modal radical perspective, terror is both a proper—even priority—research concern and an option to be considered by any serious political group. Insofar as radicals confront terrorism free from ethical or conceptual inhibitions, they encourage the full investigation of every political use of violence in this and other forms—governmental as well as oppositional, approved as well as disapproved. However, the radical (as well as the conservative) bias toward prejudging the efficacy of approved terror and inefficacy of disapproved terror must be corrected if the purposes and efficacy of terrorist violence are to be adequately researched and (predictively) understood.

*Justifications of Terror*

Selection of the terrorist option is neither blind nor whimsical. Political conflicts cannot be sustained (or even defined) in the absence of deliberation and action. In arriving at decisions, oppositional political strategists as well as their governmental counterparts rely upon (never fully complete and always to some extent distorted) information about contingencies and resources. Inevitably, their perceptions and reasoning are influenced by analytical and normative assumptions. Regardless of the "objective" adequacy of their information, conceptualization, or logic, political actors believe within the bounds of their understanding that their actions are justified. To comprehend that, their actions require taking seriously the grounds upon which those actions have been undertaken, which implies entertaining the possibility that even a terrorist (approved or not) may be objectively as well as subjectively "correct."

None of the modal criminological perspectives leads to adequate consideration of terror's justifications. Conservative blindness to approved terrorism and automatic denigration of disapproved terrorism are matched by radical eagerness to accept the justifications offered for approved terrorism and equally automatic denial of any validity to justifications of disapproved terrorism. Liberal repugnance of violence is predictably reflected in a strong tendency to construe any defense of it as a manifestation of ignorance or faulty thinking. The hypotheses that disapproved terrorists may have some justification and approved ones may not have to be given equally thorough testing if terrorist rationales are to be analytically and empirically instead of polemically evaluated.

*Terrorists as Political Actors*

Political action may be reasonably defined as behavior intended to promote or impede the acquisition or exercise of collective power. Such behavior will virtually always be in concert with other actors, given that the lone individual cannot expect success in the absence of supportive others. Within as well as among political groups, variability in levels of individual political awareness and commitment is to be expected, and in the capacity to see or accept violent tactical options. Regardless of their other attributes, including pathologies, individual terrorists cannot be understood if the relevance of their political concerns, beliefs, experiences, and relationships is not systematically determined. Even if relatively inarticulate, and perhaps on balance more criminal or sick than political, individual terrorists must be analytically linked to their respective political contexts if predictively or clinically useful explanations of their actions are to be forthcoming.

Criminological thought-ways offer little help in the effort to understand terrorists. Least helpful is the conservative insistence on attributing disapproved terrorism to pathological sources, thus shortcircuiting investigation of terrorists as political actors with variable characteristics. The liberal perspective is more helpful insofar as it does suggest the possible importance of environmental sources of terrorist thought and behavior, but it obscures the problem in conceiving the terrorist as merely an environmental victim instead of an actor within and upon a specific *political* environment. Modal radicals are unhelpful in caricaturing approved terrorists as noble warriors and disapproved ones as inhuman brutes. However, the radical perspective is nonetheless the most promising in that it implies terrorists may be authentically political actors whose socialization and selection may reflect policy decisions instead of accidents of circumstance. The key insight is that terrorists are made, not born, and may be deliberate and partly self-made creations rather than socially (or biologically, or psychodynamically) determined automatons.

*Nonrandomness of Terrorist Violence*

Terrorist violence is patterned. The occurrence and relative frequency of particular forms (bombing, armed attack, kidnapping, and so on) demonstrably vary geographically and temporally. Efforts to relate the varying incidence and prevalence of terrorist violence to environmental variables suggest that terrorism is more a function of historically generated political dynamics than of contemporary economic conditions or cultural predispositions. Initial adoption of the terrorist option appears historically most likely where political struggle has been characterized by violence and repression, reinforcing distrust of alternative modes featuring negotiation and compromise. Later, however, terrorist justifications and methods can spread through deliberate or accidental communications from one area or political group to another.

One significant consequence is that terrorism becomes increasingly difficult to understand in reference only to observable aspects of the proximate environment in which terrorist incidents occur. Another is that terrorists can become wittingly or unwittingly implicated in a widening circle of political violence that may or may not serve their original purposes, which may be adapted or subverted to aims transcending the particular interests or concerns at stake in local political settings. An adequate theory will have to encompass the many-layered reality of terrorism as an environmentally contingent yet transcendent component in the ultimately global process of political struggle.

Grasping the complex interaction among terrorism, environmental contingencies, and political dynamics is a difficult assignment from any perspective. A radical approach offers the best leads for beginning to identify historical and macrostructural sources of variation in terrorism, though the radical preoccupation with exposing the roots of disapproved governmental and oppositional terrorism might result in some confusion of analytical and polemical goals and neglect of approved terror. Liberal thinking suggests the need to be specific in identifying and measuring (estimating) relevant environmental variables, but the focus upon narrowly conceived proximate and situational factors must be greatly widened to include the historical contexts and macrostructural processes to which radical thought draws attention. Within the broad sweep of radical thinking and the structural parameters emphasized by liberal thought, the conservative perspective offers potential insights regarding cultural factors (ideology, beliefs, conceptions, information, communication channels) and their interaction with the varying aims and vulnerabilities of groups as well as individuals. Overall, each perspective offers promising leads for developing a theory integrating historical, structural, cultural, and psychological observations of the sources, mechanism, and consequences of adopting the terrorist option.

*Controlling Terrorist Violence*

Once political actors accept terrorism, their opponents face the enormously difficult problem of controlling terrorist decisionmaking and actions. The rejection of compromise is a defining characteristic of terrorist justifications, as is the firm rejection of alternatives to terror, especially nonviolent ones. The committed terrorist is an implacable enemy whose thinking is socially as well as ideologically insulated from contradicting ideas and information. Such an actor is most unlikely to be deterred by threats of imprisonment, and rarely deterred even by the prospect of torture and execution. To imprison terrorists is to give them access to either one another or potential sympathizers and recruits; to publicize their cause and elicit sympathy for their condition; to invite further attacks; and to signal current and potential terrorists that the risks are not excessive. Yet, to execute them or permit suicide is to create martyrs and reinforce the image presented in terrorist justifications of an irredeemably brutal opposition. Given any prospect that such actors may acquire the means to disseminate ever more widely their message or their model of political action, to escalate from small-scale to mass destruction, or to coerce their opponents into abandoning or contradicting accepted ethical and institutional restraints upon their own use of political violence, the need for opponents to neutralize terrorists becomes paramount.

Modal conservatives and radicals are more realistic about stopping terrorists, liberals far less so. The conservative and radical perspectives take it for granted that disapproved terrorism is to be repressed, with little or no concern about restraining the agents of repression. Liberal thought is typically hesitant about the need for repression, and encourages faith in the capacity of established legal control structures and processes to handle terrorists. If special measures are judged necessary, liberals are very likely to presume that the "exceptional" powers of control agents must and will be "temporary" and carefully delineated (administratively if not statutorily). It is to be assumed that when caught and duly convicted, terrorists will be afforded the same opportunities for rehabilitation as are other prisoners. For the modal liberal, execution is, of course, to be ruled out. In light of what is now known about committed terrorists, liberal policies are dangerously ineffectual. But such an approach does offer some leads for dealing with potential terrorists caught before "the bridge of murder" has been crossed, and perhaps for exploiting whatever ambivalence and insecurity may remain in committed terrorists.

*Preventing Terrorist Violence*

Inhibiting the perception and selection of terror as a political option is a daunting task. It may well be that "the genie is out of the bottle," that terror has become a permanent option for consideration by serious political actors. To the extent this is so, preventing adoption of the option is now more a matter of convincing opponents that alternatives are more justifiable than trying to keep them ignorant of terrorist justifications. Positive (rewarding) as well as negative (deterrent) measures are required to convince political adversaries that their survival is not threatened and that their interests are better served by minimally violent and certainly nonterrorist actions.

A liberal perspective offers the most realistic positive leads; conservative thinking is the most realistic in suggesting negative measures; radical thinking is the least realistic. Positive measures encouraged by liberal thought emphasize improving opportunity structures and "safety nets" to inhibit indigenous terrorism, while also helping to improve ("develop") foreign environments conducive to terrorism and its export. Less promising and rather naive are liberal anticipations regarding the impact of interpersonal contact and protolerance programs. Conservative toughness is promising for developing negative measures to prevent terrorist violence. More effectively monitoring immigration, travel, foreign contacts, and communications would obstruct both imported (transnational, international) and indigenous terror. Campaigns to promote traditional conceptions of morality and patriotism might have some utility, but only insofar as such conceptions fit the environmental realities and political needs of a very wide range of diverse populations—a decreasingly likely accomplishment. Radical utopianism offers little other than a naive faith in the likelihood and potential impact of revolutionary social changes. Still, fostering the expectation of a better life to come may in the long run be the ultimate preventive measure.

## A Composite Approach

Terrorism is a major but so far unmet challenge to prevailing models of reality in conservative, liberal, and radical thinking about crime. A critical appraisal of the three basic perspectives, hypothetically applied to explaining and confronting terrorism, has revealed or suggested not only shortcomings but also the potential contributions of each. The next step is to bring together the more promising features of each perspective in a hybrid approach that generates sensible propositions for both research and policy consideration. Systematic development of the following outline is necessarily a project requiring more time, space, research, and collegial assistance.

1. It is assumed that violence is a political resource and that the terrorist option is perceived.
2. The terrorist option is more likely than possible alternatives to be adopted under one or more of the following conditions:
    a. The political actor has supporting others. (Terrorism is collective, not idiosyncratic.)
    b. The political actor and supporting others have directly or vicariously experienced political violence. (Any predispositions to political or other violence is learned.)
    c. The political experience of the political actor and supporting others has been characterized by the perceived ineffectiveness of alternatives to terrorist violence. (Alternatives have been considered, probably tried, and subsequently rejected.)
    d. The political actor and supporting others believe that adoption of the terrorist option is justified both ethically and tactically. (Ethical compunctions about using terrorist violence are neutralized by invoking both "higher good" arguments and tactical considerations. The more objectively demonstrable are the justifications, the more likely is the terrorist option to be adopted.)
3. Imported terrorist justifications are more likely to encourage than to create indigenous terrorism. (People who expect their lot to improve, or at least not to worsen, are more likely to reject justifications of terror than are the hopeless and distressed.)
4. The initial purposes of committed terrorists are more likely to be subordinated to other interests or concerns under one or more of the following conditions:

a. Terrorists are dependent for support upon others not committed to their particular cause. (Dependency corrupts: client terrorists are more likely than independent ones to modify their calculations and actions so as to meet the tacit or explicit expectations of their patrons.)

b. Exported terrorist violence occurs within their political setting with their knowledge, and especially if with their cooperation. Cooperation, whether passive or active, leads to altering one's goals and actions so as to avoid operating at cross-purposes and to enlist support.)

c. They participate as consultants or operatives in political struggles other than the one in which they are first involved. ("Professional" terrorists are more likely than personally involved ones to become more and more insensitive to their own initial political concerns, and to degenerate into either mercenary opportunism or unreasoning nihilism.)

5. The incidence, prevalence, and forms of terroristic violence depend more upon terrorists' calculations of opportunities, risks, resources, and impact than upon socioeconomic conditions or cultural attitudes toward violence. (Terrorists operate where, when, and how the perceived chances of success are greatest. Publicity and shock value outweigh in their decisions the risks of becoming casualties.)

6. Committed terrorists must be killed without ceremony to be controlled. (Public legal nonlethal responses are markedly less likely to curtail terrorist violence than are minimally publicized extraordinary, though authorized lethal measures. Such authorized "summary justice" must be effectively subjected to strict internal accountability, and not be public or legally restrained. Only a very few carefully selected and trained authorized agents should be used. Counterterrorist violence by anyone else must be strictly prohibited and suppressed. To the degree that such safeguards are lacking, assassination of terrorists will be counterproductive in discouraging consideration of nonviolent options and increasing oppositional violence.)

7. Imported (including sponsored) terrorist violence can be reduced more by negative than by positive measures; the converse is true for indigenous terrorist violence. (Imported terrorism is unresponsive to manipulation of proximate environmental conditions. Indigenous terrorism is responsive insofar as positive measures are effectively implemented and their success communicated. International governmental, or "state-sponsored," terrorism is harder to control or prevent than indigenous terrorism, but easier to control than prevent.)

Only the skeleton of a theory has been displayed; it will be fleshed out elsewhere. For now, my hope is that this attempt will stimulate other criminologists to transcend conservative, liberal, and radical thinking to accept the challenge of developing empirically grounded theories and policies regarding what may be the greatest criminal threat of our age: political terrorism.

## References

*Annals of the American Academy of Political and Social Science* 463. 1982. Special issue on international terrorism. September.

Crenshaw, Martha, ed. 1983. *Terrorism, Legitimacy, and Power: The Consequences of Political Violence.* Middletown, Conn.: Wesleyan University Press.

Currie, Elliott. 1985. *Confronting Crime: An American Challenge.* New York: Pantheon.

Freedman, Lawrence Zelic, and Yonah Alexander, eds. 1983. *Perspectives on Terrorism.* Wilmington, Del.: Scholarly Resources.

Gibbons, Don C. 1979. *The Criminological Enterprise: Theories and Perspectives.* Englewood Cliffs, N.J.: Prentice-Hall.

Gibbons, Don C., and Peter Garabedian. 1974. "Conservative, Liberal, and Radical Criminology: Some Trends and Observations." In *The Criminologist: Crime and the Criminal,* edited by C.E. Reasons, pp. 51-65. Pacific Palisades, Calif.: Goodyear.

Gurr, Ted Robert, ed. 1980. *Handbook of Political Conflict: Theory and Research.* New York: Free Press.

Han, Henry Hyunwood, ed. 1984. *Terrorism, Political Violence and World Order.* Lanham, Md.: University Press of America.

Inciardi, James A., ed. 1980. *Radical Criminology: The Coming Crises.* Beverly Hills, Calif.: Sage.

Kerstetter, Wayne A. 1983. "Terrorism." In *Encyclopedia of Crime and Justice,* edited by Sanford H. Kadish, 4: 1529-36. New York: Free Press,

Laqueur, Walter. 1977. *Terrorism: A Study of National and International Political Violence.* Boston: Little, Brown.

Miller, Walter B. 1974. "Ideology and Criminal Justice Policy: Some Current Issues." In *The Criminologist: Crime and the Criminal,* edited by C.E. Reasons. Pacific Palisades, Calif.: Goodyear.

Schmid, Alex P. 1983. *Political Terrorism.* New Brunswick, N.J.: Transaction Books.

Turk, Austin T. 1983. "Assassination." In *Encyclopedia of Crime and Justice,* edited by Sanford H. Kadish, 1: 82-88. New York: Free Press.

——. 1982. *Political Criminality: The Defiance and Defense of Authority.* Beverly Hills, Calif.: Sage Publications.

Vold, George B., and Thomas A. Bernard. 1986. *Theoretical Criminology.* 3d ed. New York: Oxford University Press.

Wardlaw, Grant. 1982. *Political Terrorism: Theory, Tactics, and Counter-Measures.* Cambridge: Cambridge University Press.

Zimmerman, Ekkart. 1983. *Political Violence, Crises and Revolutions: Theories and Research.* Cambridge, Mass.: Schenkman.

# 3

# The Poverty of Theory in Corporate Crime Research

*Donald R. Cressey*

During the Watergate scandal and the overseas-payments scandal of the 1970s, executives of most large U.S. corporations wrote or revised codes of conduct for their company managers, officers, and other employees.[1] A study of 119 of these codes found all but one trying to convince readers that the author has good reasons to ask them to behave legally and ethically (Cressey and Moore, 1980, 1983; Cressey, 1982). Some authors asked for ethical behavior because, they prophesied, the free-enterprise system will go under if business personnel continue to use unethical means for accumulating profits.[2] Other authors asked corporation personnel to be honest because, they said, dishonesty is bad for the reputation of the firm. Still others simply claimed that virtue is its own reward or evoked the authority of Moses, Christ, or Abraham Lincoln in an effort to convince members of their firm that they should be ethical.

Of most relevance to criminological theory about crime causation were admonitions based on the author's assumption that the corporation is a person who, like other persons, has obligations under a social contract. Sheared of its philosophical, political, and sociological complexities, the social-contract principle declares that civilized life exists only because citizens subordinate their personal interests to the interests of the larger society: a social contract or covenant gives each citizen a duty to behave responsibly and ethically toward fellow citizens. In the codes of conduct, as in both popular and professional writings, this principle often is expressed in an analogy with sports, resulting in assertions that "the rules of the game" must be honored in the processes and procedures by which profits are accumulated (Friedman, 1962:15).

The authors of the conduct codes often expressed the moral of such assertions in terms suggesting that a social contract determines the duties of employee-citizens to the collectivity that is the corporation: each employee has obligations to the corporation and to fellow employees. ("Don't steal from the company or from other workers.") Less commonly, admonitions about following the "rules of the game" were based on the assumption that a social contract puts limits on the methods that the corporation managers, directors, officers, employees and agents can legitimately use to maximize their firm's income. ("Don't commit crime on behalf of the company").

Of special significance to criminological research and theory pertaining to so-called organizational crime and corporate crime was a third notion, namely, that a social contract ("rules of the game") also limits the behavior of corporations. Here, the social contract is assumed to involve relationships among a society's corporate citizens as well as among its biological ones. That is, the corporation itself, not its personnel, is viewed as the actor. As I just reported, each corporation is considered a person who, like real persons, has ethical and legal obligations to the collectivity. Such anthropomorphism was most clearly expressed in discussions of "corporate social responsibility" and in sentences such as "good corporate citizenship demands business conduct that is both lawful and ethical" (Cressey and Moore, 1980:22). A cogent example appeared in a recent letter to the editor of the *Wall Street Journal*: "Adolph Coors Co. is a leader in re-cycling aluminum and certainly wants to be a good corporate citizen in all parts of the country" (Kenny, 1986).

Such conceptions of corporations' duties under the social contract are consistent with the legal fiction that a corporation is a person and the concordant legal fiction that this artificial person is capable of committing a crime. Criminologists frequently display deep commitment to the notion that fictitious Americans, like natural ones, should live up to the legal and ethical obligations inherent in the social covenant. They do so when discussing their conceptions of "organizational crime" and "corporate crime," as well as when calling for "corporate social responsibility" and for more severe punishment of corporate wrongdoers. It seems timely to ask whether this commitment is self-defeating because it is based on the erroneous assumption that organizations think and act, thus saddling theoretical criminologists with the impossible task of finding the cause of crimes committed by fictitious persons.[3]

Note that the criminologists who developed the corporate crime and organizational crime concepts (Geis, 1962; Clinard and Quinney, 1973; Schrager and Short, 1978; Gross, 1978, 1980; Clinard and Yeager, 1980), like the corporation executives who characterized corporations as persons in their codes of conduct, have joined the ranks of a wide range of professional personnel, social scientists, and ordinary citizens who make organizations talk, act, think, and otherwise behave just like real people. Nowadays, we accept without question newspaper reports saying that Procter and Gamble has put a new product on the market, or that Exxon is searching for oil in the Santa Barbara Channel. "The White House said today" is heard on the television news almost every evening. Newspapers regularly carry stories saying that corporations and agencies have "decided," "declared," "claimed," and "agreed." Consumers object to form letters saying that the computer made a mistake when it sent the gas bill, but they nevertheless tell their friends that "the gas company" has erred. After the trial of the Ford Motor Company for reckless homicide in 1980, a juror who voted "not guilty" said that he nevertheless thought the Pinto was a reckless automobile (Clinard and Yeager, 1980:261)[4].

Consistently, social scientists have written volumes on "organizational behavior." They have done so because it is easy to assume that corporations and other organizations act like humans. Sociologists and experts on business administration say, for example, that corporations and other formal organizations formulate goals and the means to achieve them, just as do human members of committees, teams, and other action groups. Political scientists assert that states, legislatures, and court systems make decisions and seem to have lives of their own. Public administration specialists insist that cities behave, as do their police dep rtments, fire departments, and sewer departments. Historians studying foreign relations treat entire nations as corporations when they analyze actions of "the United States," not of Americans. Anthropologists and sociologists say they can observe the behavior of societies and cultures themselves, not just the behavior of a society's members or of the participants in a culture. And economists, of course, have projected the characteristics of a rational, calculating "economic man" onto many organizations, ranging from mom-and-pop grocery stores to entire nations. To them, the corporation is an ideal "economic man" because it persistently pursues profits and, ideally, lets nothing distract it from that pursuit.

Criminologists, being interdisciplinary, do and say all of these things, and more. For example, a recent review of an important book on controlling white-collar crime anthropomorphized as follows: "Corporations do after all have consciences, and they can be pricked by publicity. That is the conclusion of this first-rate study by two Australian legal scholars" (Maitland, 1986). I myself have asserted that juvenile gangs (Sutherland and Cressey, 1978:196-98), La Cosa Nostra "families" (Cressey, 1969), and even prisons (Cressey, 1965), as well as corporations (Cressey, 1976) and other organizations, behave as units, like persons. More significantly, criminologists rather routinely, unthinkingly, and erroneously assert that corporations have the psychological capacity to be guilty of crime and to suffer from punishment. Assuming such a capacity is what, after all, makes it possible for criminologists to hold that corporations, as corporations, ought to follow ethical and legal "rules of the game," thus displaying social responsibility.

For at least a century, U.S. courts have regarded every corporation as a person. This legal fiction is essential to fairness. For example, if corporations were not assigned the legal characteristics of persons, no one could sue them or make contracts with them. And if corporations were not said to reside in a city, state, and nation—as do persons—they would be "outlaws" in the true sense of the word, for no government would have jurisdiction over them. A citizen could not even be employed by a corporation if the corporation were not viewed as a person who lives somewhere and has a right to make contracts and otherwise conduct business.

But anyone who tries to understand white-collar crime is severely handicapped by the fiction that corporations are disembodied political, social, and economic persons who behave just like ordinary men and women. As Arthur Selwyn Miller, the noted constitutional law scholar, has said, "The corporation is obviously more than a person, however characterized in law" (Miller, 1968:9). This assertion can be validated by making just two commonsense observations.

In the first place corporations are allowed to do many things persons are not permitted to do. They can buy and sell each other legally, as though the "person" being bought or sold were a slave. (According to the October 4, 1985, issue of the *Wall Street Journal*, "Revlon agreed to go private by selling itself for $56 a share, or about $1.77 billion.") They also can exterminate each other legally by methods resembling those of homicidal maniacs (cutthroat competition).

In the second place the makeup of a corporation is quite different from the makeup of a human being. For this reason, corporations can do things that are not humanly possible: growing from infant to adult in a year, shrinking from giant to midget, merging two or more bodies into one, achieving immortality on earth.[5]

Even more relevant to criminologists is the fact that legal fiction notwithstanding, the corporation is obviously *less* than a person. It cannot learn, contemplate, feel guilty or proud, intend, or decide. For this reason, none of the social machinery—including the social contract—that controls real persons has any effect on corporations. Writing ethical codes, preaching social responsibility, noting the wisdom of the Golden Rule, or even depicting the horrors of hellfire and damnation that await evil persons can have no influence on fictitious persons who do not have the psychological makeup of real ones.

These observations about the nature of the corporation have some counterparts in everyday life. For example, auditors and accountants call corporations "entities," which is another name for "things," not "persons."[6] And even though the language of ordinary citizens endows corporations with human attributes, this language also suggests that everyone knows the difference between a "person" and a "thing." Thus, the gas company is never referred to as "she" or "he." It, like other companies, is always called "it." This usage characterizes legal language too, suggesting that the regulation of corporations might be more effective if corporation codes of ethics as well as regulatory laws pertained to the real persons in charge of inanimate objects, not to the objects themselves.

Everybody knows that automobiles really do not behave, even if "Motor Vehicle Codes" and "Automobile Safety Rules" imply that they do. (Out west, we even have a California Auto Body Association.) Motorists, pedestrians, legislators, police, court officials, jail officials, and criminologists all recognize that the reference in such codes and rules is to drivers and passengers, not to cars. Similarly, a citizen who is indignant about an incorrect gas bill will, sooner or later, attribute the error to humans. "The bastards at the gas company don't know what they are doing," the victim of a bureaucratic snafu is likely to claim. In other bailiwicks, too, people with common sense recognize that "entities" do not behave. Saying that the United States has declared war is recognized as just a shorthand way of saying that the president and a majority of the members of Congress have decided to go to war. Reports stating that the White House has spoken, that the city of New York has made a decision, or that a police department has changed its tactics also are readily recognized as poetic license, as a lazy observer's way of substituting vagueness for needed precision, or as a canny reporter's way of concealing true authorship of the actions.

Although criminologists cannot be expected to crack down on all the poetic license in the world, it is time for them to put their common sense to work when confronting reports indicating that a corporation or other organization has committed a crime. Typical of such reports is a statement recently made by Representative John D. Dingell (Associated Press, 1985). In a five-page letter to Defense Secretary Caspar W. Weinberger, Dingell accused two huge corporations of conspiring to cheat a third organization, the U.S. Air Force:

> General Dynamics knew full well that the Air Force had already paid Westinghouse for the development of these tools. This is not sloppy business

practice on the part of General Dynamics—it is fraud. The entire acquisition was clearly double-billed. It is fraud on the part of Westinghouse to plot with General Dynamics. It is also not the finest hour of the Air Force for having allowed this to happen.

In real life, if not in the academic world, criminologists realize that such anthropomorphism is misleading. Firms really do not "know," "plot," and "allow," as the legislator's statement suggests. They are "entities" that are owned, managed, and administered by *people*. Each of these persons talks, decides, intends, agrees, disagrees, deliberates, buys, sells, works, thinks, estimates, errs, and otherwise behaves. Each can be coerced by threats of punishment and persuaded by promise of reward. Except for the few who, due to mental disability, cannot tell right from wrong, each is responsible for individual actions, including violations of the penal code. The corporation itself does not behave. It just sits there. Its so-called actions are but manifestations of actions by real persons, as Hayworth argued years ago (1959), and as the Australian Trade Practices Act, enacted in 1974, makes abundantly clear:

> Any conduct engaged in on behalf of a body corporate by a director, agent or servant of the body corporate or by any other person at the direction or with the consent or agreement (whether express or implied) of a director, agent or servant of the body corporate shall be deemed, for purposes of this Act, to have been engaged in also by the body corporate [quoted by Hopkins, 1978:226].

The main criminological complication is this: to say that a real person rather than a corporation made a decision or acted in a certain way is to say that this individual should be held responsible for the costs as well as the benefits of the decision. Under this procedure corporations would commit no crimes—*executives* who commit the crimes now called crimes of corporations would be arrested, prosecuted, and convicted. This seems reasonable in light of the fact that executives and others whose decisions and behavior make money for the corporation, not the corporation itself, are praised and rewarded when total profits soar. On the other side, however, the policy unreasonably asks law-enforcement officers to detect the crimes of executives who are masters at using the corporate form to mask their misbehavior. As Jack Katz (1980) has noted, it also unreasonably asks prosecutors to convict managers who skillfully use the corporate entity to make their criminality almost impossible to prove.[7] Finally, a former United States attorney has correctly observed that corporations are often prosecuted because it would be unjust to try to establish the criminal liability of "individuals who, under normal standards of prosecutorial discretion, should not be prosecuted" (Martin, 1985). This is not meant to imply, however, that conviction of corporations is an easy matter, even under strict liability statutes (Shudson, Onellion, and Hochstedler, 1984).

Against these practical complications must be weighed the intellectual cost to criminology of the existence of a category of criminal behavior that criminologists' causal theories cannot explain. Although it is possible to find significant correlations between rates of corporate crime and structural variables, such as industry, financial status, and size, it is not possible to go beyond these statistical relationships to statements about causation. Most damaging is the fact that there can be no social psychology of so-called corporate or organizational crime because corporations have no biological or psychological characteristics. I pointed out a quarter of a century ago (Cressey, 1960) that an effective model of crime causation must have two parts: a statement about the way crime is distributed in the social order, and a logically consistent statement about the social psychological process by which criminal behavior is manifested. The latter is necessarily missing in explanations of so-called corporation crime or organizational crime. For reasons of expediency, it might be necessary for legislators, prosecutors, and judges to maintain that imaginary persons commit crimes. But it does not make sense for scientists to maintain that these fictitious persons do so because they are in poverty, are frustrated, are labeled as troublemakers, have poor attachments to the social order, or have had an excess of associations with criminal behavior patterns. Clearly, corporate criminality cannot be explained by the same causal principles used to explain the criminality of real persons.

The work of criminological pioneer Edwin H. Sutherland is especially revealing in this regard. Sutherland invented the concept of white-collar crime and introduced criminologists and others to white-collar criminality. He declared that his motive was "to reform the theory of criminal behavior, not to reform anything else" (1949:v). His discovery of white-collar crime, he said, showed that the theories of crime causation that were in favor during the 1930s and 1940s—theories stressing personal and social pathologies—are defective because they pertain, at most, to working-class criminals alone. Accordingly, he developed a new causal theory—differential association and differential social organization—that made sense of the crime of high status persons as well as those of poor people.

It is rather ironic to find, therefore, that Sutherland considered corporations as persons but did not so much as give a hint about how the differential association process, a process of learning, could affect them. There is a great difference between what Sutherland said and what he did (Cressey, 1976). He defined white-collar crime as "a crime committed by a person of respectability and high social status in the course of his occupation," but he studied the crime rates of *corporations*, not of live persons. His writings show that he viewed the executives of corporations as persons who are respectable and of high social status and, thus, as white-collar criminals if they violated the law in the course of their duties as executives. But the same writings show that Sutherland frequently but rather casually treated corporations as high status persons too, just as did the authors of the codes of ethics described earlier (Hopkins, 1980).

As Geis pointed out long ago, "The major difficulty in *White Collar Crime* as criminological research lies in Sutherland's striking inability to differentiate between the corporations themselves and their executive and management personnel" (1962). For example, Sutherland's demonstration of the relevance of differential association theory to white-collar crime begins with a discussion of documents relating to how businessmen are inducted into illegal behavior by other businessmen (1949:234-41). But soon the discussion moves to diffusion of illegal practices, and here the object of inquiry is corporations, not business personnel. Sutherland unthinkingly attributes human capabilities to these corporations: "When one firm devises (an illegal method) of increasing profits, other firms become aware of the method and adopt it, perhaps a little more quickly and a little more generally if the firms are competitors in the same market than if they are not competitors" (1949:241). He never asked the significant theoretical question, "By what process does a firm 'become aware of' and 'adopt' illegal processes?" Had he done so, he would have been reminded that humans behave but entities do not.

Vacillation between concern for the criminality of business personnel and the criminality of anthropomorphized corporations also appears in Sutherland's discussion of the psychological characteristics of offenders. This discussion appears, significantly enough, in a chapter entitled "Variations in the Crimes of Corporations" (1949:257). Sutherland first notes that corporations, being fictitious, obviously cannot suffer from human psychiatric disorders such as feelings of inferiority, regression to infancy, and Oedipus complexes. Then he assaults his own common sense by assuming that as corporations commit crimes they do so without acting through their officers, directors, employees, or agents. This assumption comes as he shows that variations in the crime rates of individual corporations are associated with variations in the positions of these corporations in the economic structure and then argues that the corporations, not their executives, are the significant actors:

> Manufacturing and mining corporations seldom violate laws regarding advertising because they seldom engage in advertising for sales purposes. This variation in practices is related to the position they hold in the economic

structure rather than to the personal traits of the executives of the corporations . . . p. 262 Two facts are especially significant. First, many corporations
violate the antitrust law in certain industrial areas and not in others, although
the officers and directors are the same in all these areas . . . That is, behavior
as to violations of law varies without variations in persons involved in the
behavior. Second, many corporations which violated the antitrust law forty
years ago are still violating that law, although the personnel of the corporation
has changed completely. That is, variations in persons occur without variations in behavior as to the antitrust law [1949:264]. p. 264.

Sutherland's materials on the criminal careers of businessmen suggest
that a corporation's crimes are but manifestations of the crimes of its
executives. In retrospect, it seems incredible that he did not use these
materials in his discussions of what is now known as corporate crime or
organizational crime. The fact remains, however, that he did not formally
attribute similarities and consistencies in law violation among corporations to socialization into criminal behavior of new executives by old ones,
as Marilynn Cash Mathews recently did (1984).[8] Such attribution is consistent with the theory of differential association and differential social organization.

It appears that *White Collar Crime* has become an influential criminological classic as much because Sutherland anthropomorphized corporations as because he defined white-collar crime as crime committed by
persons of respectability and high social status. The work showed that the
prevailing causal theories were incorrect, being based on biased samples,
but it really was not much of a theoretical contribution. Thus, as I just
indicated, Sutherland neglected to show how differential association or any
other social psychological process might possibly work to produce criminal
conduct in the fictitious persons called corporations. His macrolevel (sociological, epidemiological) hypothesis that rates of corporate crime are
associated with structural conditions, such as position in the economic
world (differential social organization), seems reasonable enough. But that
is as far as one can go when the object of study is not a human being.

By drawing a distinction between "occupational crime" and "corporate
crime," Clinard and Quinney (1973) tried to reduce the confusion introduced by Sutherland. The former was defined as "violation of the criminal
law in the course of activity in a legitimate occupation," so that, in fact,
only some occupational crime is white-collar crime in the Sutherland sense
of "crime committed by a person of respectability and high social status in
the course of his occupation." Occupational crime differs from corporate
crime principally in that it consists of "offenses committed by individuals
for themselves in the course of their occupations and the offenses of employees against their employers," and corporate crime consists of "the of-

fenses committed by corporate officials for their corporation and the offenses of the corporation itself" (1973:188).[9] Braithwaite consistently de-
fines corporate crime as "the conduct of a corporation, or individuals
acting on behalf of the corporation, that is proscribed by law" (1982:1466).

Note that these definitions of corporate crime really show no concern for
the differences between corporate crimes committed by persons and crimes
committed by organizations. In their recent monumental work, Clinard
and Yeager seem to correct this defect by deleting "corporate officials"
from the definition: "A corporate crime is any act committed by corporations that is punished by the state, regardless of whether it is punished
under administrative, civil, or criminal law" (1980:16). Almost imme-
diately, however, they reintroduce Sutherland's ambiguity by going back to
the idea that corporate crime also is perpetrated by real persons:

> Corporate and occupational crime can be confused. If a corporate official
> violates the law in action for the corporation it is corporate crime, but if he
> gains personal benefit in the commission of a crime against the corporations,
> as in the case of embezzlement of corporate funds, it is an occupational crime
> [1980:18].

This blurring of the distinction between corporate crimes committed by
persons and corporate crimes committed by organizations asks theoreticians to use one causal theory to explain both, an impossible task. The
meddling is reflected in much of Clinard and Yeager's prose, just as it is in
Sutherland's. For instance, in a single paragraph these authors first discuss
"corporations whose executives have knowingly concealed" unsafe products or occupational hazards, and then give two examples: (1) "Firestone
officials knew that they were marketing a dangerous tire in their radial
'500s.'" (2) "Allied Chemical also knew from its own laboratory research
that Kepone is a potential carcinogen. It went ahead and marketed the
deadly substance anyway." The first example reports on real people, the
second on a fictitious person. But then Clinard and Yeager blur the distinction even more by using the plural *their*, not *its*, to refer to a corporation's
possessions: "Many workers were subsequently poisoned, and miles of
Virginia's James River ruined due to Allied's dumping of their Kepone
wastes" (1980:10-11). This compromise nicely avoids the question of
whether the action was that of the corporation or of corporation executives.

Clinard and Yeager's one short reference to organizational crime also
blurs the distinction between crimes by persons and crimes by organizations: "Corporate crime actually is *organizational* crime occurring in the
context of complex relationships and expectations among board of direc-

tors, executives, and managers, on the one hand, and among parent corporations, corporate divisions, and subsidiaries, on the other" (1980:17). Consistently, their chapter on corporate organization and criminal behavior (pp. 43-73) vacillates between the view that the corporation (or parts of it) is a rational actor and the view that so-called corporate actions actually are the actions of managers. When the latter view prevails, causal explanation of executive criminality is stressed, and "the making of a corporate criminal" is said to be a matter of socialization of subordinates by elites (differential association). When the corporation itself is considered the actor, Clinard and Yeager's stress is on explaining crime rates, and variation in them is attributed to organizations' differing economic and political environments. This explanation is not very nourishing: "Economic pressures and other factors operate in a corporate environment that is conducive to unethical and illegal practices" (1980:132).[10]

Sutherland's vacillation between concern for the criminality of business personnel of respectability and high social status and the criminality of anthropomorphized corporations also has been duplicated in the writings of several other sociologists. The most noteworthy of these, perhaps, is Edward Gross, a distinguished scholar who specializes in the study of organizations, not crime. In an attempt to educate criminologists on the subject of organizational crime, Gross asserts that "all organizations are inherently criminogenic" (1978:56). In documenting this theoretical assertion, he shifts back and forth between the notion that organizations commit crimes and the notion that organizational personnel commit them. On the one hand, he says, "there is built into the structure of organizations an inherent inducement for the *organization* itself to engage in crime" (1978:56). On the other hand, he insists that organizations do not behave: "Although organizations are here held to be criminogenic and although courts no longer exhibit much hesitation in charging the organization itself with crime, organizations of course cannot themselves act—they must have agents who act for them" (1978:65).

Once people accept the fiction that organizations behave, they tend to promote it. Gross is no exception. His principal point is one adapted from Hayworth (1959), namely that an organization may be considered as acting when "what is meant is that the organization is *responsible* for the outcome" (1980:59). But a corporation is not responsible, at least in the sense of the criminal law, until the law declares it to be a person. Moreover, even if events represent the outcome of the patterns of activities that make up the "behavior" of this fictitious person, and even if the quality of the outcome "depends minimally on the peculiar qualities of the [biological] persons who make it possible," as Gross put it (1980:59), the fact remains that biological persons are responsible for establishing and maintaining the patterns and, thus for the action. "If [a human] were to arrange the workers differently, something different would happen," Gross concedes. But he then argues, in contradiction, that organizations, not humans, commit crimes because they require that persons be able to implement criminal patterns and then socialize them in ways such that they become willing to do so. He attributes all of this to the performance emphasis found in complex organizations, saying that when organizations (not people) face difficulty in meeting their profit goals they resort to crime. His criminological theory, then, is a simple one: poverty causes crime.

After presenting this macrolevel theory, Gross turns to the social psychological processes involved as the "agents" (corporation executives) of organizations come to commit crimes. Again, his key idea is that criminality stems from stress on performance and goal attainment. Ambitious, shrewd, and morally flexible managers are most likely to make it to the top, Gross says, and these are the persons who commit crimes on behalf of corporations (1978:71). Moral flexibility is especially significant, he continues, because socialization to the attitudes, values, and behavior patterns of successful superiors is the active crime producing process. But this idea, which is consistent with differential association theory, is soon garbled because, to Gross, the demand for a nondemanding moral code is made by an anthropomorphized organization, not by the corporation executives he has been discussing. Managers are socialized to change their moral beliefs, he says, "so that they match whatever is called for by the organization" (1978:69).[11] But organizations, being only entities, do not make demands; people do.

At the beginning of the follow-up essay (1980) Gross seems to correct his error by noting once more that organizations cannot act:

> Although the law has created these "persons," they cannot, of course, act autonomously; agents must act for them. Hence when we speak of corporate "actors" it must be recognized that there are always biological persons who act, in the manner of puppeteers, to put the show on the road [1980:54].

Still, Gross insists, a theoretical problem of disentangling people and organizations remains (1980:52). His proposed disentanglement is rather snarled, however, because it includes the legal fiction that corporations are persons and, moreover, that these persons "run afoul of the law" even if they do not deliberately break it (1980:52). More generally, corporations "take on lives of their own" (1980:58), and corporate crime follows from their need to create an orderly market (1980:53), their ways of integrating persons (1980:61), and their performance emphasis (1980:64). Consistently, Gross describes Staw and Szwajkowski's study of antitrust law violations

(1975) and then concludes: "When these organizations faced difficulty in meeting their profit goals, they resorted to crime in order to do so" (1980:64; also see Gross, 1978:57).

Sets of organizations, such as sports leagues, cartels, trusts, industries, and oligopolies, also are clothed with the attributes of people: "The organizations not only know of one another's existence, their own success depends further on a continuous monitoring of one another's behavior" (Gross, 1980:69). The crime of price fixing, too, is discussed as though it were an arrangement between organizations, not people: "The companies seem to have tacitly recognized that once they get into a battle about prices, they can easily destroy each other" (1980:70). But a U.S. attorney, noting that corporations can act only through their officers, directors, employees or agents, has come to a more realistic conclusion: "Corporations don't commit crimes, people do" (Martin, 1985).[12] In one famous case illustrating this point, Robert L. Crandall, president and chief operating officer of American Airlines, suggested in a telephone conversation with Howard Putnam, president of Braniff Airways, that price fixing might solve the financial problems that both were experiencing: "I think it's dumb as hell ... to sit here and pound ... each other and neither of us making a [word deleted] dime," Crandall said. When Putnam asked, "Do you have a suggestion for me?" Crandall replied, "Yes, I have a suggestion for you. Raise your goddam fares 20 percent. I'll raise mine the next morning. ... You'll make more money and I will too" (Rothbart, 1983).

A profound criminological problem is raised by Gross's, Clinard and Yeager's, Sutherland's, and many others' blurring of the distinction between crimes committed by corporations and crimes committed by executives and other managers. This is the problem of intentionality. In courthouses, the rise of the legal fiction that corporations commit crimes gave a severe jolt to the traditional criminal-law principle that performing an outlawed act does not alone make the doer guilty of crime. The actor also must have intended the act to be a crime. The legal fiction also stops theoretical criminologists in their tracks because it undermines every social psychological theory about the causation of crime that has been formulated and every theory that might be formulated in the future. Even if corporations are called persons for purposes of arguments, these juristic persons—unlike real people—cannot have criminal intentions.[13] It is not unreasonable to conclude that the corporation therefore is incapable of committing a crime (Mueller, 1957; Velasquez, 1983). But this logical conclusion is not drawn in the criminal courts and, as we have seen, it is not drawn by some criminologists either.

Some people unthinkingly claim that corporations deliberately commit crimes. A science reporter, for example, recently used the following language to describe a case involving the Eli Lilly Company: "According to the Justice Department, Lilly was fully aware of, but delayed telling U.S. authorities about, ten cases in which patients taking Oraflex had suffered fatal or debilitating liver or kidney disease" (Marshall, 1985). Sometimes people hold, alternatively, that corporations are guilty of crimes even if they are incapable of formulating criminal intent. For example, the just-quoted reporter also says, "On 21 August, Eli Lilly & Co. wrote to its stockholders to say that it had negotiated an end to a federal investigation that 'puts to rest any speculation regarding intentional misconduct on the part of the company' in the marketing of Oraflex, an arthritis medicine suspected of causing liver and kidney failure . . . Lilly's strong emphasis [was] on the fact that it was guilty only of 'technical misdemeanors'."

The Lilly Company could be guilty of "technical misdemeanors" even if no one intended to do wrong because legislatures have enacted statutes which hold persons, including fictitious corporate ones, liable for certain crimes, even if there is no psychological state such as criminal intent or *mens rea*. These strict liability statutes modify the ancient legal principle holding that, by definition, every crime involves an intentional act. Appelate courts have ruled that such statutes are constitutional, despite their radical character.

The best example of a strict liability crime is murder under the felony-murder doctrine of criminal law. Under the rule of strict liability (called "straight liability" in British courts), if someone dies because the defendant committed a felony, the defendant is guilty of murder. For example, a defendant who intentionally committed arson in order to defraud an insurance company is guilty of murder if a firefighter dies trying to knock down the flames. So far as murder is concerned, the defendant's intent is not considered. Another example is so-called statutory rape. If a man has sexual intercourse with a girl who is beneath the age of consent, he is guilty of a crime, even if she eagerly cooperates. He is strictly liable. The fact that he might have believed the girl to be of legal age is not officially considered. Criminal intent or *mens rea* is not an element of statutory rape.

Corporations, not being real persons, cannot intentionally commit crimes such as larceny, murder, or even fraud. Accordingly, most of the crimes said to have been committed by them are, like felony-murder and statutory rape, strict liability offenses. This means that the corporation is held criminally liable for the offense if the offense occurs.

Consider, for example, violations of the Sherman Antitrust Act of 1890, a law that stipulated that "every contract, combination in the form of trust or otherwise, or conspiracy in restraint of trade" is a crime (misdemeanor) punishable by a fine of $5,000. At first federal judges took this statement literally, and corporations were held strictly liable for their violations. But then, as I have shown elsewhere, the "rule of reason" came to replace strict liability; this was a way of insisting that criminal intent must be present before there can be a finding of guilt (Cressey, 1976:225). For example, what appellate courts were fifty years ago calling a "conscious parallelism" in the pricing of products by "competing" corporation executives was not taken to be evidence of "conspiracy in restraint of trade." The U.S. attorney general at the time (1937) complained that the courts refused to adopt the only practical criterion of restraint of trade—price uniformity and price rigidity—and insisted, instead, on trying to determine whether a fictitious personality has an evil state of mind.

The substitution of an evil intent for strict liability made it difficult to convict corporation executives of violating the Sherman Act, and it made it all but impossible to convict corporations themselves. Probably the substitution was made because, in the cultures of federal courthouses, there was, and is, a sympathetic understanding of corporations and their executives. But it is possible, too, that judges have resisted holding corporations guilty under strict liability statutes because they believe that courts have a duty to defend the traditional principle that an act is not criminal unless the actor intended it.[14] Even today, "monopolizing" in violation of antitrust law must be "nasty monopolizing" to be illegal; "no-fault" (strict-liability) restraint of trade is not enough (Clinard and Yeager, 1980:137-38).

Sutherland's treatment of criminal intent and strict liability is consistent with, but just as confusing as, the fact that he defined white-collar crimes as crimes committed by real, high-status persons but conducted his research on the crimes of fictitious persons called corporations. On the one hand, he argued that corporations or corporation executives (he was not clear about which of these he had in mind) intend at least some fraudulent ("patently false") advertisements: "For example, an advertisement of gum-wood furniture as 'mahogany' would seldom be an accidental error and would generally result from a state of mind which deviated from honesty by more than the natural tendency of human beings to feel proud of their handiwork" (1949:42). On the other hand, he noted that due to strict liability statutes, white-collar crime is like ordinary crime in the sense that a showing of criminal intent is not required in all prosecutions of either kind of crime. "The important consideration here," he said, "is that the criteria which have been used in defining white collar crime are not categorically different from the criteria used in defining some other crimes" (1949:41).

This consideration governed Sutherland's research on the crimes of corporations. He did not acknowledge, in *White Collar Crime* or elsewhere, that most if not all the laws violated by the seventy corporations he studied had strict liability provisions. More important, he did not even speculate about how differential association theory might make sense of criminal behavior that was not intended by a real person, let alone by a juristic one. As already noted, no social psychological theory can make sense of behavior that is not intended, be it an ordinary crime such as felony murder or a white-collar crime such as restraint of trade, false advertising, or unfair labor practices.

Schrager and Short have recently walked in Sutherland's footsteps on this issue (1978). The legal literature teams with discussions of criminal intent, strict liability, and corporate criminal liability (Hall, 1982: 266-94). By and large, however, Schrager and Short's discussion of organizational crime ignores the criminological implications of these discussions. They note, clearly enough, that "the white-collar crime perspective does not deal adequately with unintended consequences of organizational behavior," but they do not really remedy this in their discussion of "organizational crimes," defined as "illegal acts committed by an individual or a group of individuals in a legitimate formal organization, which have a serious physical or economic impact on employees, consumers or the general public" (1978:411-12). This because they first make the puzzling claim that strict liability is rarely used in criminal prosecutions, follow that with an assertion that "lack of intention is typical of organizational offenses having physical consequences" (1978:409-10), and then assert further that the law's requirement of criminal intent is met by their definition's stipulation that, to be organizational crime, the action must be committed in accordance with the operative goals of the organization (1978:412).

There are at least three fuzzy points in their definition and their commentary on it. First, *crime* and *criminal* are technical legal terms. Behavior cannot be a "crime" unless it is in violation of criminal law, meaning that it has been declared to be punishable by the state. And, as I have already noted, if a man does not intend his harmful act and if statute holds him strictly liable for the act, then his behavior is not an "illegal act" or an "offense"—at least not a criminal one—because he is not guilty. Obviously, it therefore cannot be an "organizational crime."

Second, the last part of Schrager and Short's definition is gratuitous because no act is a crime unless it does harm of some kind. "Serious physical or economic impact" is a characteristic of all felonies. Schrager and Short seem not to have noticed that violations of occupational health and safety regulations, for example, do not always have a *serious* impact but are crimes nevertheless. The issue is not one of seriousness. It is one of whether the offense is properly called "organizational."

Finally, to discern that an act was performed in accordance with organizational goals—as Schrager and Short's definition of organizational crime requires—is to deal with the legal problem of motivation, not of intent. That this is an error can be made obvious by use of a fictitious, but illustrative, case: Suppose the leaders of a terrorist organization announce that one of their operational organizational goals is to overthrow the government of the nation in which they reside. They agree that they need automatic weapons to do so. Suppose, further, that three members of the organization, hearing of a machine gun for sale, plot a bank robbery in which they will work as a three-person team to pull off the job. Then they harm the bank's investors by robbing them of $23,142.33, and they use the money to buy the gun. Now the *intent* of each of these three members was to rob. The *motive* of each was to acquire some money that could be used for revolutionary purposes, in accordance with the announced operational organizational goals. Each of the three is guilty of robbery and, perhaps, conspiracy, but the motive for the robbery and conspiracy is not what makes them guilty.

To underline the importance of the distinction between intent and motive, suppose that after the robbers in this fictitious case have been arrested, convicted, and sent to prison, they send a note to the editor of *Crime and Social Justice* asserting they are political prisoners. The assertion is based on the fact that their robbery was carried out in accordance with the operative goals of their organization, which are political in nature. At law, however, they are not political criminals or "organizational criminals," for that matter. Their crime was very much unlike the crime of political criminals who have violated laws stating, for example, that "harming the patriotic interests of the people" is punishable by imprisonment. Moreover, their motive (to get money with which to advance their political cause) could not have been officially taken into consideration by the judge or jury deciding their guilt. Instead, a judge or jury necessarily found that their intent was to rob, and a combination of this *mens rea* and a harmful act, prohibited by law, is what got them convicted. If motives were used to determine guilt, as Schrager and Short seem to recommend, then anyone whose motives were not acceptable to judge or jury would be guilty of organizational crime.

It could be argued that all this law talk is beside the point because Schrager and Short are merely saying, in a fuzzy way, that criminological theorists ought to (1) note that organizational crime is an important variety of white-collar crime, itself not a legal category, and then (2) use the organizational criminals' motives ("in accordance with the operative goals of the organization") to explain their behavior. I have been criminology's principal proponent of the notion that this kind of explanation is consistent with differential association theory and ought to be encouraged (Cressey, 1954). But Schrager and Short actually do not use the concept of organizational crime in this social psychological way. This is clear in their discussion of intentionality. They want to shift the focus of inquiry *away* from motives, such as "I kept my mouth shut about the dangerous design of the brakes because I knew the boss would fire me if I didn't," and *toward* the objective characteristics of criminal acts. Significantly, this shift would make organizational crimes into strict liability offenses which are not explainable in differential association terms or in any other social psychological framework:

> In view of the often impenetrable difficulty of evaluating the motives behind illegal organizational actions, the definition shifts the focus of inquiry to the objective characteristics of these actions. The logic is similar to that employed in the legal concept of strict liability, which holds an offender responsible for illegal behavior without regard to the existence or absence of *mens rea* (a guilty mind) [Schrager and Short, 1978:412].

In conclusion, let it be said that it is just as ridiculous for criminologists to try to explain criminal behavior that was not intended as it is for judges to try to determine whether a fictitious person has an evil state of mind. Because corporations cannot intend actions, none of their criminality can be explained in the framework of behavioral theory. It is time for criminologists to eradicate this embarrassment by acknowledging that corporation crimes and organizational crimes are phantom phenomena. Such acknowledgment will not lead to abandoning criminological concern for white-collar offenses and offenders. On the contrary, the strength of this area of criminological research and theory will grow in proportion to the degree to which criminologists first recognize that only real persons have the psychological capacity to intend crimes, and then focus their analytical and theoretical skills on these persons.

Auditors and other accountants have already found an appropriate name for much of the behavior in question: management fraud.[15] This is deliberate deception by managers that injures others through misleading financial statements (Elliot and Willingham, 1980:4). Fraud of this kind is by definition perpetrated by corporation executives and other managers rather than by organizations. It is committed on behalf of corporations, not against them. For example, income obtained for firms by means of price fixing, bribery, and false advertising as well as profits obtained for firms by means of industrial pollution of air and water, violations of labor laws, and the manufacture and marketing of dangerous products are all maintained or increased by use of false (and thereby fraudulent) books and records. The techniques that managers use to commit crime on behalf of corporations are the same as those used by embezzlers to commit crimes against corporations. (For an illustration, see Clinard and Yeager, 1980:162). The verbalizations (motives) probably are the same in both cases, too (Cressey, 1980). Robert Elliot and John Willingham, partners in one of the world's largest auditing firms, have noted that there is a practical reason for determining why such behavior is so widespread: "Management frauds are of primary importance in the family of business improprieties because to a large extent the health of the capital markets rests on confidence that financial statements are not fraudulent. Thus, the detection and prevention of fraudulent financial statements goes to the heart of the functioning of the economy" (Elliot and Willingham, 1980:viii).

Despite my emphasis on explaining the criminality of biological persons, not of fictitious ones, I am not here proposing that corporations do not commit crime. Criminologists, like everyone else, must use the only permissible definition of crime, the legal one. This means that criminologists must accept the fact that the criminal law treats corporations as persons and says that these persons commit crimes.

What I am proposing is that criminologists acknowledge that no theory dealing with crime causation can make sense of strict-liability criminality or any other criminality that is not intended. Corporations and organizations, being inanimate, cannot formulate criminal intent. Accordingly, as Geis pointed out a quarter of a century ago, "For the purpose of criminological analysis ... corporations cannot be considered persons, except by recourse to the same type of extrapolatory fiction that once brought about the punishment of inanimate objects" (1962:163).

It is not reasonable to try to locate the cause of unintentional, accidental, behavior that is called murder under the felony-murder doctrine. By the same token, it is not reasonable to try to identify the cause of crimes that are said to be committed by organizations. These crimes are by definition exceptional to any behavioral theory. Once criminological theoreticians acknowledge that fact they will be able to concentrate more attention, time, and energy on the question of why managers steal for the company as well as from it. As Michael Levi has put it, "There has been much sententious discussion of the need for an organizational perspective in the analysis of corporate crime, but adequate theorizing must mediate organizational norms through individual actors who make decisions ... " [1985:45].

## Notes

1. I thank the following persons for comments made on an earlier draft, which was presented at the Annual Meetings of the American Society of Criminology, San Diego,November 14-16, 1985: David Biles, Marshall B. Clinard, Gilbert Geis, Peter N. Grabosky, Andrew Hopkins, Ronald C. Kramer, Marilynn Cash Mathews, Dario Melossi, Calvin Morrill, James D. Orcutt, and Diane Vaughan.
2. This prophecy also was made by Clinard and Yeager (1980:325).
3. Many philosophers, including French (1979), Donaldson (1982), and Meyers

(1983) have argued that corporations can and should be held morally responsible for their actions, which are said to be intentional. Although this argument seems relevant to the question of why corporations came to be viewed as persons, it sheds little light on the possibility that the actions, especially criminal ones, of corporations are not intentional and are in fact the actions of individuals. Other philosophers insist, as I do, that it is a mistake to view a corporation either as a monolithic agent that acts like an individual person or as a single autonomous moral agent that is distinct from its members. A philosopher who is a leading authority on business ethics has made this point succinctly and well:

> Corporations are composed of individuals and they "act" only if those individuals are moved to act. Consequently, no sanction will be effective unless it touches and moves those individuals within the corporation who are ultimately and really responsible for what the corporation does [Velasquez, 1985:38].

4. Here are two additional examples of such anthropomorphism. (1) In his "On Language" column in the February 17, 1985, *New York Times Magazine*, William Safire quoted Israel's former defense minister, Ariel Sharon, as saying, "I came here to prove that *Time* lied." (2) Richard Reeves's July 25, 1985, column in the *Santa Barbara News-Press* was headed, "Too many people give in to 'White House' demands." Reeves noted that some 200 people have the technical authority to dial a number and say, "This is the White House calling." He went on to note that "there is something inherently dangerous in the system, because 'the White House' is just a bunch of retired stockbrokers, journeymen public relations men, smart lawyers and ex-colonels, none of them politically accountable for their judgments."

5. In the famous *Dartmouth College* case, decided by the Supreme court in 1819, Chief Justice John Marshall commented on the immortal character of corporations as follows: "Among the most important [properties of corporations] are immortality, and, if the expression may be allowed, individuality; properties by which a perpetual succession of many persons are considered the same, and may act as a single individual" [*Dartmouth College v. Woodward*, 17 U.S. 518 (1819)].

6. Ironically enough, auditors nevertheless treat their own firms as persons, not as entities. Stockholders reading the annual reports of corporations rarely note that the signatures following the auditors' statements are obviously fictitious; the reports are "signed" by firms such as Peat, Marwick, Mitchell & Company rather than by a real auditor. In accepting such reports about or by fictitious persons, we overlook the fact that in each case a real person or group of persons has made a decision.

7. According to newspaper accounts, the indignation of members of Congress about the recent E.F. Hutton scandal stemmed principally from their belief that the white-collar police officers in the U.S. Department of Justice could not detect crimes by any corporate executive, even though the corporation pleaded guilty to 2,000 crimes, or from their belief that the prosecutors in Justice either could not or would not prosecute either low-level personnel who executed the crimes or high-level executives who knew or should have known what their subordinates were up to (Pasztor, 1985).

8. Sutherland often made this attribution in conversations and correspondence,

however. For example, in a letter written to Frederic M. Thrasher on September 18, 1944, Sutherland said:

> Up to the present time I have done very little work on case histories of white-collar criminals but have made studies of corporations rather than of persons. The paper which I gave in Chicago was a statistical analysis of records of courts and administrative commissions as to the 70 largest industrial and commercial corporations in the U.S. (excluding the petroleum corporations, and also public utilities and financial corporations). I am enclosing a tabulation of the results. . . . The persons responsible for the actions on which courts and commissions made decisions against the corporations are the executive officers and the boards of directors. They include persons such as John D. Rockefeller, J.P. Morgan, Henry Ford, Julius Rosenwald, Harold Swift, etc.

But then Sutherland vacillates, just as he was to do in *White Collar Crime*, published five years later:

> My general inclination is to conclude that the criminal record of a corporation is a function of its opportunity to violate the law rather than of the personnel concerned. This makes big business an area of criminal culture, so far as the laws covered are concerned, with everyone participating who has been subjected to that culture, provided he has opportunity.

9. Five years after the appearance of Clinard and Quinney's publication, Andrew Hopkins of the Australian National University could discern that it had a bandwagon effect: "Most writers . . . use the term [corporate crime] to refer to crime committed by the corporation itself or on behalf of the corporation by its employees, in furtherance of the corporate interest" (1978:214). Similarly, Georges Kellens of the University of Liège, Belgium, recently declared, "It is generally accepted now that white collar crime designates acts committed against business, for instance a computer fraud within a company, while organizational crime means acts committed by business against others" (1985:15).

10. Reference to vague "pressures," "factors," "forces," and "tensions" is a popular way of "explaining" corporate crime, be it the crimes committed by executives or those said to be committed by organizations. Clinard and Yeager write about "pressures" on management and "forces" driving executives to violate the law. They use one or the other of these words seven times on the first several pages of a discussion of managers' illegal behavior (1980:273-76). Gross also accounts for executive misconduct with these atmospheric concepts (1980:64), which are synonymous for ignorance about the actual schedules of rewards and punishments that are used by people to modify other people's behavior.

Here, Clinard and Yeager's attempt to account for variations in the crimes said to be committed by corporations is obviously weak and uninformative because they rely on the same mystical "pressures" and "factors" that they use to account for crimes perpetrated by managers. Other criminologists who use these terms have produced equally lame "explanations" of why corporations violate the law. Diane Vaughan, for example, asserts that organizations seek economic success by unlawful means because they experience "pressures" to make money and also experience "social pressures" to stay in business (1983:62). She also uses "factors," "tensions," "structural factors," and "structural tensions" (p. 67) to refer to these "pressures" for organizations to engage in "unlawful organizational behavior." In addition, she says, "structure, processes and transactions systems" are "factors" that "create opportunities for organizations to act as offenders" (p. 68). Further, she insists, the "regulatory environment" also is a "factor" in violation (pp. 96,101).

In the world of "pressures," "forces," and "factors" there is no causality, so much uncritical use of atmospheric and hydraulic concepts can only lead to the conclusion that crime can be forever studied but never explained. Vaughan draws this conclusion, thus displaying an attitude of scientific despair shared by many criminologists:

> The conditions and combinations of factors that do or do not result in unlawful behavior cannot yet be unraveled. They cannot, therefore, be discussed in the language of causality, but rather in terms of factors that facilitate, generate, encourage, or present opportunities to attain resources through unlawful conduct [1983:68; also see Vaughan, 1986].

11. Vaughan, too, erroneously insists that organizations, not executives, socialize employees: "The tendency for organizations to select members like those already there, to devote resources to socializing employees ... produces employees willing to act in the organization's behalf" (1986:7). Her discussion of policy implications nevertheless seems consistent with criminological theory that locates the cause of criminal behavior in social learning and differential social organization: "In order to alter the behavior of individuals, policy must aim at altering structural determinants of individual choice: the competitive environment, organizational characteristics, and the regulatory environment" (1986:12).

12. William Safire, the famous columnist, agrees with Martin but notes the negative implications for general deterrence. In a column titled "Companies Don't Swindle Banks, People Do," he refers to the 1985 scandal in which "a gang of E.F. Hutton & Co ... systematically bilked tens of millions of dollars out of 400 banks." Safire goes on to disagree with Attorney General Edwin Meese, who had announced that conviction of the company "makes it clear that white-collar crime will not be tolerated." "On the contrary," Safire concluded, "the pretense that no human beings operate E.F. Hutton makes it clear to the business world that if your company is shot through with managers involved in a huge swindle, the Meese Justice Department will limit the liability to the corporation. None of the guilty officers will have to pay" (Safire, 1985).

13. Behaviorists, including the author, do not accept routine assumptions about the effects on human behavior of mentalistic mechanisms such as "mind" and "will." I long ago tried to show (Cressey, 1953, 1954) that a person's attempts to achieve a criminal goal (called "intentions" in the criminal law) are linguistic rather than mentalistic, as are the person's reasons for such action ("motives"). At criminal law the defendant's intent ("I am going to kill my neighbor") but not the defendant's motive ("because he let his dog run in my garden") is officially considered by judges and juries as they make decisions about guilt. Considerations of motives is officially permissible only when deciding on the proper sentence for persons who have been found guilty.

14. In our culture, with its emphasis on due process of law, citizens demand that they be notified in advance of the precise nature of any deviation that is punishable by state officials so they can avoid it. When strict-liability statutes

make them criminally liable for behavior that they could not avoid or in some other way did not intend, they are righteously indignant. Accordingly, strict-liability statutes must be administered very gingerly. Pollner (1970, 1979) long ago showed, for example, that traffic-court judges find it necessary—in the interest of justice—to let persons who are guilty under strict-liability statutes enter unofficial but exonerating pleas of "guilty with excuse." By the same token judges seem to look with a fishy eye at strict-liability statutes that ask them to hold even fictitious persons criminally liable for behavior that was not intended by any person, real or fictitious.

15. The term was coined in the later 1970s by Stanley Sporkin, then chief of the enforcement section of the Securities and Exchange Commission.

## References

Associated Press. 1985. "Military Contract Fraud Charged." *Santa Barbara News-Press*, November 22.

Braithwaite, John. 1982. "Enforced Self-Regulation: A New Strategy for Corporate Crime Control." *Michigan Law Review* 80: 1466-1507.

Clinard, Marshall B., and R. Quinney R. 1973. *Criminal Behavior Systems: A Typology*. 2d ed. New York: Holt Rinehart & Winston.

Clinard, Marshall B., and P. Yeager. 1980. *Corporate Crime*. New York: Free Press.

Coffee, John C. 1977. "Beyond the Shut-Eyed Sentry: Toward a Theoretical View of Corporate Misconduct and an Effective Legal Response." *Michigan Law Review* 63: 1127-47.

Cressey, Donald R. 1953. *Other People's Money: A Study in the Social Psychology of Embezzlement*. Glencoe, Ill.: Free Press.

———. 1954. "The Differential Association Theory and Compulsive Crime." *Journal of Criminal Law, Criminology, and Police Science* 45:49-64.

———. 1960. "Epidemiology and Individual Conduct: A Case from Criminology." *Pacific Sociological Review* 3:847-58.

———. 1965. "Prison Organizations." In *Handbook of Organizations*, edited by James G. March, pp. 1023-70. Chicago: Rand McNally.

———. 1969. *Theft of the Nation: The Structure and Operations of Organized Crime in America*. New York: Harper & Row.

———. 1976. "Restraint of Trade, Recidivism and Delinquent Neighborhoods." In *Delinquency, Crime and Society*, edited by J.F. Short, Jr. Chicago: University of Chicago Press.

———. 1980. "Management Fraud, Accounting Controls, and Criminological Theory." In *Management Fraud: Detection and Deterrence*, edited by R.K. Elliott and J.J. Willingham, pp. 117-47. New York: Petrocelli.

———. 1982. "Self-Regulation in the Control of White-Collar Crime." *Revue Internationale De Droit Penal*, 1e and 2e trimestres, pp. 73-87.

Cressey, Donald R., and C.A. Moore. 1980. *Corporation Codes of Conduct*. New York: Peat, Marwick, Mitchell Foundation.

———. 1983. "Managerial Values and Corporate Codes of Ethics." *California Management Review* 4:53-77.

Donaldson, Thomas. 1982. *Corporation and Morality*. Englewood Cliffs, N.J.: Prentice-Hall.

Elliott, Robert K., and J.J. Willingham. 1980. *Management Fraud: Detection and Deterrence.* New York: Petrocelli.

French, Peter A. 1979. "The Corporation as a Moral Person." *American Philosophical Quarterly* 16:207-15.

Friedman, Milton. 1962. *Capitalism and Freedom.* Chicago: University of Chicago Press.

Geis, Gilbert. 1962. "Toward a Delineation of White-Collar Crime Offenses." *Sociological Inquiry* 32:160-71.

Gross, Edward. 1978. "Organizational Crime: A Theoretical Perspective." In *Studies in Symbolic Interaction*, vol. 2, edited by D. Denzin. Greenwich, Connecticut: JAI Press.

_____. 1980. "Organizational Structure and Organizational Crime." In *White-Collar Crime: Theory and Research*, edited by G. Geis and E. Stotland. Beverly Hills, Calif.: Sage Publications.

Hall, Jerome. 1982. *Law, Social Science and Criminal Theory.* Littleton, Colo.: Rothman.

Hayworth, L. 1959. "Do Organizations Act?" *Ethics* 70:59-63. (Cited by Gross, 1980.)

Hopkins, Andrew. 1978. "The Anatomy of Corporate Crime". In *The Two Faces of Deviance*, edited by J. Braithwaite and P. Wilson. Brisbane, Australia: University of Queensland Press.

_____. 1980. "Controlling Corporate Deviance." *Criminology* 18:198-214.

Katz, Jack. 1980. "Concerted Ignorance: The Social Psychology of Cover-up." In *Management Fraud: Detection and Deterrence*, edited by R.K. Elliott and J.J. Willingham. New York: Petrocelli.

Kellens, Georges. 1985. "Economic Crime: Some Priorities for Research." In *Economic Crime: Programs for Future Research*, edited by D. Magnusson. Stockholm: National Council for Crime Prevention.

Kenny, P.J. 1986. "Keeping Tabs on Beer Cans." *Wall Street Journal*, May 27, p. 29.

Levi, Michael. 1985. "A Criminological and Sociological Approach to Theories and Research into Economic Crime." In *Economic Crime: Programs for Future Research*, edited by D. Magnusson, pp. 32-72. Stockholm: The National Council for Crime Prevention.

Maitland, Ian. 1986. Review of *The Impact of Publicity on Corporate Offenders* by Brent Fisse and John Braithwaite. *Contemporary Sociology* 15:380-81.

Marshall, Eliot. 1985. "Guilty Plea Puts Oraflex Case to Rest." *Science* 229:1079.

Martin, John S. 1985. "Corporate Criminals or Criminal Corporation?" *Wall Street Journal*, June 19.

Mathews, Marilynn Cash. 1984. "Corporate Crime: External vs. Internal Regulation." Ph.D. dissertation, University of California, Santa Barbara.

Meyers, Christopher. 1983. "The Corporation, Its Members and Moral Accountability." *Business and Professional Ethics Journal* 3:33-44.

Miller, Arthur S. 1968. *The Supreme Court and American Capitalism.* New York: Free Press.

Mueller, Gerhard O.W. 1957. "Mens Rea and the Corporation." *University of Pittsburgh Law Review* 19:21-50.

Pasztor, Andry. 1985. "Bell's Probe of Illegal Overdrafts Is Disputed by Lawmakers, Regulators." *Wall Street Journal*, September 13.

Pollner, Melvin. 1970. "On the Foundations of Mundane Reasoning." Ph.D. dissertation, University of California, Santa Barbara.

_____. 1979. "Explicative Transactions: Making and Managing Meaning in Traffic Courts." In *Everyday Language: Studies in Ethnomethodology*, edited by G. Psathas, pp. 227-48. New York: Irvington.

Rothbart, Dean. 1983. "American Air, Its President, Get Trust Suit Voided." *Wall Street Journal*, September 14.

Safire, William. 1985. "Companies Don't Swindle Banks, People Do." *Santa Barbara News-Press*, May 12.

Schrager, Laura Shill, and J.F. Short, Jr. 1978. "Toward a Sociology of Organizational Crime." *Social Problems* 125:407-19.

Shudson, Charles B., Ashton B. Onellion, and Ellen Hochstedler. 1984. "Nailing an Omelet to the Wall: Prosecuting Nursing Home Homicide." In *Corporations as Criminals*, edited by E. Hochstedler, pp. 128-56. Beverly Hills, Calif.: Sage Publications.

Staw, Barry M., and E. Szwajkowski. 1975. "The Scarcity-Munificence Component of Organizational Environments and the Commission of Illegal Acts." *Administrative Science Quarterly* 19:345-94.

Sutherland, Edwin H. 1949. *White Collar Crime*. New York: Dryden, 1946.

Sutherland, Edwin H., and Donald R. Cressey 1978. *Criminology*. New York: J.B. Lippincott.

Vaughan, Diane. 1983. *Controlling Unlawful Organization Behavior*. Chicago: University of Chicago Press.

_____. 1986. "Organizational Misconduct: The Connection between Theory and Policy." Paper read at the Annual Meetings of the Law and Society Association, Chicago.

Velasquez, Manuel. 1983. "Why Corporations Are Not Morally Responsible for Anything They Do." *Business and Professional Ethics Journal* 3:1-18.

_____. 1985. Comment on "The Hester Prynne Sanction" by Peter A. French. *Business and Professional Ethics Journal* 4:35-38.

# 4

# A Propensity-Event Theory of Crime

*Michael Gottfredson and Travis Hirschi*

An increasingly obvious shortcoming of criminology is that it lacks a general theory to guide social policy in the area of crime treatment and prevention. Since the Great Society programs of the 1960s, and the deinstitutionalization movement of the 1970s, no criminological theory can claim responsibility for important elements of public policy about crime. The area has thus proved attractive to those promoting such theory-free policies as selective incapacitation, career criminal programs, neighborhood watch, police sting operations, and preventive patrol. In the meantime criminology has pursued research devoted to such antitheoretical problems as theory integration, the application of cookbook "causal models" to available data, and the creation of social-psychological interpretations of the demographic facts about crime. Criminology textbooks list all current theories as though they were equally valuable, equally useful, and at the same time equally easy to criticize, so that the net impression is that all ideas about crime, including those of the readers, are as good as all others. None of which does much to promote consistent or useful thinking about crime.

All too often the solution criminology offers for these problems is to collect more data, usually via the large-scale longitudinal study, data meant to represent the interests of several disciplines. Typically, the role of biology, economics, and psychology in the causation of crime and delinquency is acknowledged, but the analysis ends up focusing on one or another of the traditional sociological correlates of crime (e.g. peer delinquency), and the interpretation rests on one or another of the traditional sociological theories of criminal motivation. In sociological criminology, there is little room for such concepts as temperament, personality, deterrence, choice, or opportunity. Theories in the field continue to see offenders as driven by

57

crime-specific forces over which they and society have no control. As a result, crime continues to be something about which little can be done without fundamental change in the offender or in the structure of society.

In this paper we attempt to move toward a theory of crime that acknowledges the ability of society to control crime without fundamental reconstruction of itself or the individuals within it. This theory allows input from diverse disciplines and is owned by none of them. It yields concrete predictions about the implications of various crime policies.

### Crime and Criminality

We begin with a distinction between two important concepts: crime, an event, and criminality, a characteristic of persons (Hirschi and Gottfredson, 1986).[1] Theories of criminality should tell us why some people are more prone than other people to commit crimes. Theories of crime should tell us the conditions under which criminal propensities are likely or unlikely to lead to crime. Theories of criminality are likely to be faulty unless they explicitly take into account the slippage between propensity and action; theories of crime are likely to be faulty unless they properly estimate the role of the "criminal" in such activities. Put another way, the distinction between crime and criminality reminds us that crime is only one of many possible expressions of "criminality," and that crime requires more than criminals for its existence. For example, some people are more likely than others to seek risk or excitement. Such propensities may lead to the commission of criminal acts. They may also lead to accidents, abuse of alcohol, or to promiscuous sexual behavior. They may also lead to gambling, auto racing, and downhill skiing. The assumption of a one-to-one correspondence between the propensity to commit crime and the occurrence of crime, although standard throughout criminology, is, according to our view, at best misleading. The correlation between committing crimes, using drugs, smoking, being in accidents, and gambling is sufficiently high that a single underlying propensity must be common to all of them. Explication of the sources and consequences of this propensity is the specific task of a theory of criminality.

It is also misleading to assume that crimes are a perfect or even a good reflection of the tendencies of the person. General propensities manifest themselves in a variety of ways, and often have only a weak relation to specific events that they indeed cause. Criminologists often express awareness of this fact, but they tend to do so in a negative, even destructive way. For example, it is frequently alleged that some such trait as "aggressiveness" is not a cause of crime because aggressiveness can also be useful in such noncriminal activities as business, sports, and politics. The assumption that a general trait must have a specific manifestation in criminal acts before it can be a cause of crime is wrong. The only logical requirement is that persons possessing the trait be more likely than persons lacking it to commit criminal acts. The trait can, and often will, show itself in noncriminal activities as well. We would not say that strength has nothing to do with the likelihood that one will become a boxer because it also may show itself in weight lifting, bricklaying, or football. By the same token, we cannot conclude that adventuresomeness has nothing to do with crime because it may also show itself in a variety of noncriminal activities. The contribution of such traits is also obscured by the fact that they are by no means necessary conditions for crime. A highly risk aversive person will, given the prospects of great financial benefit, sometimes engage in larceny. And even the most risk aversive person will, given great provocation, sometimes use physical force. But the existence of crimes contrary to the tendencies of those committing them is not evidence that the tendency is irrelevent to crime causation. On the contrary, the infrequency of such cases is evidence of its power or importance.

What we propose, then, is the separation of two often confused concepts (Hirschi and Gottfredson, 1986). Crimes are short-term, circumscribed events that presuppose a peculiar set of necessary conditions (e.g. activity, opportunity, adversaries, victims, goods). Criminality, in contrast, refers to stable differences across individuals in the propensity to commit criminal or theoretically equivalent acts.

## A Theory of Criminality

We now have good evidence to suggest that differences in the propensity to engage in criminal acts are established before the high-crime-rate years, persist during those years, and indeed maintain themselves throughout life. The traits we have in mind in making this statement (e.g. aggressiveness, impulsivity, self-centeredness, intelligence) can be measured independently of and prior to the commission of criminal acts. The fact that they predict criminal acts correctly suggests that they predict themselves even better, that they are highly stable over the portion of life on which data are available.

As noted, such traits do not ineluctably lead to crime, regardless of the setting in which the individual is located. To complicate things further, these traits themselves often affect the settings in which the individuals possessing them are located, e.g. the amount of education they obtain, the kind of job or marriage they achieve, the area of the city in which they live. Despite these complications, indeed to begin to understand them, the field needs the concept of criminality, and its explication must be the focus of a theory that would begin to understand crime.

In our view the criminality dimension is best understood for current purposes as a consequence of inadequate child rearing practices. We focus on child rearing because of the empirical evidence that criminality can be predicted from the quality of family life at an early age (Glueck and Glueck, 1950; West and Farrington, 1977; McCord, 1979; Patterson, 1980). Although there is good reason to believe that some of the traits relevant to criminality have a biological as well as a social basis, the evidence suggests to us that biological factors have less influence on crime than child rearing practices (see Mednick and Christiansen, 1977). We provisionally hypothesize that this is because biological traits are more general and therefore more neutral with respect to crime than are socially caused sources of variation. For example, *activity level* is crime relevant but not crime specific, and is probably more genetic than social (Buss, 1975). In contrast, *impulsiveness* is crime relevant and crime specific but probably more social than genetic. We begin then with the hypothesis that socially produced traits are more closely correlated with crime than are more purely biological factors. The source of a trait does not, however, bear on the logic of its connection to crime. Our argument is that in all cases the connection is the same, that is, the trait makes crime more likely but does not require it.

To understand the concept of criminality as a stable tendency of individuals originating in the early stages of development, it is necessary to skip ahead to the acts that high levels of criminality make more likely. Crimes are acts of force or fraud that cause pain, suffering, or loss on the part of others. Such acts take time and energy, often strength or cunning, and are thought to result in punishment of the offender if he or she is detected. Crimes offer something of immediate benefit to the offender, whether psychic or pecuniary, but cannot be in general a realistic source of lasting income or pleasure. Other events or activities share some but not all of the characteristics of crime, and are therefore also influenced by (or are indicators of) criminality, for example, use of alcohol or drugs, tardiness at school or job, slothfulness, fast and reckless driving, tattooing.

Given the nature of the effect, we are in a position to describe its causes. Obviously, persons prone to crime tend to be active, relatively strong, unconcerned for the suffering of others, indifferent to punishment, impulsive, pleasure oriented, and reckless. As indicated in the discussion of the distinction between "social" and "biological" traits relevant to crime, such traits need not share a common cause or be strongly correlated with each other. Certainly some intercorrelation would be expected, however, especially for some traits. For example, such "antisocial" or "crime-relevant" characteristics as lack of concern for others, impulsivity, pleasure orientation, recklessness, and immunity from punishment suggest a fair amount of shared variation. A source of the intercorrelation among the traits of criminality is the fact that those appearing early tend to generate those appearing late. For example, impulsiveness and hyperactivity tend to produce school failure, which in turn heightens recklessness, immunity from punishment, and impulsiveness. In fact, we might make the general point that these traits tend to perpetuate themselves by producing situations consistent with their manifestation. (For example, lack of concern for others tends in the long run to put the individual in situations where he or she is free to act without concern for the opinion of others.)

The origins of criminality in child rearing suggest that criminality is more or less naturally present, that it requires socialization for its control. Presumably, the more biologically based traits bear on the ease with which socialization can take place. The aggressive, active, adventuresome child will be more difficult to socialize, and will obviously require more rather than less skill, attention, and care on the part of the parents. But because the parents will tend to share the child's traits, they will be less likely to be able to perform the required socialization tasks. (In addition, they will be less likely to be around when socialization is most critically required.) The theory thus requires no positive explanation for criminality. It assumes that in the absence of socialization the child will tend to be high on crime potential.

When the child high on crime potential enters school, he or she brings along traits contrary to the demands of the school setting (Cohen, 1955). Teachers and other school authorities may, in principle, do what the parents have failed to do, but the prospects for reversal are not good. The school demands competence, concentration, self-denial, attention, obedience, and respect for others. Failure to meet these demands results eventually in exclusion from the system, such that it can no longer function as a substitute agency of socialization. At this point criminality probably reaches its maximum value.

The idea of a general propensity toward crime is not new. It has been around criminology from the beginning, and continues to resurface under a variety of names. The need to assume that offenders carry with them a tendency toward crime is apparently matched by the desire among criminologists to deny such an assumption, to make offenders products of the instant situations in which they find themselves. Personality assumptions are, in fact, favorite targets of criminological theory and research (e.g. Schuessler and Cressey, 1950), and at any given time the dominant position in the field seems to be that such assumptions are contrary to logic and evidence. Most theories of "crime" start with the assumption that offenders are the same as nonoffenders. These theories do not typically confront the problem that they themselves go on to identify factors that make offenders measurably different from nonoffenders (e.g. labeling, strain, cultural values, "learning"), such that the assumption of initial similarity is transformed into the assumption of eventual differences in propensity. Because all theories make this assumption, the question is "when" the relevant differences can be identified and what produces them, not whether they exist. Because all person theories require the assumption of stable differences among people, it seems to us illogical for advocates of one theory to criticize advocates of other theories on these grounds. The sources of differences, and their stability, are empirical questions. The fact of difference is the basis of theorizing in the first place, a fact that is not altered by its alleged disciplinary sources.

## A Theory of Crime

Crimes are events. They take place at particular points in space and time. For crimes to occur, many things may be necessary, only one of which is the presence of a potential offender. Each crime will have its own set of necessary conditions. Fortunately for the purposes of theory, all crimes appear to be attractive to persons high on criminality—not because crimes are crimes but because the pleasures they provide are consistent with the traits comprising criminality. Thus, for example, purse snatching yields excitement and sometimes at least a little money, both of which make the event "worthwhile" to those capable of performing the act, which requires strength and speed, and a short-term orientation and little planning. Similarly, ordinary check fraud requires little more than blank checks, an interest in money, and lack of concern for potential embarrassment. It is often assumed that more serious crimes, such as homicide and rape, require special motivation not covered in the concept of criminality. The evidence says otherwise. "Rapists" and "murderers" turn out, on inspection, to be a cross-section of ordinary offenders. Their crimes require no modification of the ideas presented here.

If particular crimes do not require unique offender explanations, it follows that all crimes satisfy the demands of criminality, that all persons, especially those high on criminality, are potential offenders. It follows further that the offender can for some purposes be ignored in explaining crime. Crimes require an object or person capable of gratifying the offender. They require a sense of immunity from painful consequences or a sense that these consequences do not outweigh the gratification the act will provide (see, generally, Cohen and Felson, 1979; Hindelang et al., 1978).

Some of the conditions necessary for crime are aspects of the external environment, that is, they are to a large degree independent of the characteristics of the potential offender. These conditions include the availability of goods to be stolen, damaged, or burned, and persons to be assaulted or defrauded. Other external conditions bear on the sense of immunity experienced by the offender, such things as darkness, anonymity, and vulnerability of the victim.

Other conditions cannot easily be classified as external or internal because they involve simultaneous consideration of characteristics of the potential offender and the external environment. For example, body build is known to be correlated with the commission of criminal acts, presumably because large-strong potential offenders have a sense of security vis-à-vis small-weak victims. By the same token, gang members are more likely to engage in certain criminal acts, presumably at least partly because the group provides them with an advantage relative to some victims.

Still other characteristics of potential offenders may be related to crime because they reflect criminality and crime at the same time. For example, the use of alcohol is governed in part by those characteristics indexing criminality, and this is probably the principal reason for the association between alcohol consumption and crime. (Cigarette smoking has much the same relation to crime.) At the same time, alcohol may also increase the probability of some types of crime independent of the criminality of the offender because it relates to emotionality, sense of immunity, or lack of motor control. School failure makes for probable unsupervised time during the day when houses are unoccupied and thus more suitable targets for burglary. School failure thus indexes criminality (lack of persistence and competence) and also increases the likelihood of crime over and above that to be expected from the criminality of the offender.

This theory is attractive to many disciplines, but is not owned by any of them. Because it does not envision the causes of crime to be solely properties of the environment, it can freely accept the variation research has shown to be due to differences among individuals. Because it does not envision the causes of crime to be solely properties of the individual, it can freely accept the variation research has shown to be due to differences among environmental conditions. We have elsewhere outlined the advantages of this perspective for multidisciplinary work (Hirschi and Gottfredson, 1988). In fact, it is easy to see that the concept of criminality is readily compatible with the assumptions of some theories within all disciplines. Thus, for example, social-control perspectives from sociology and psychology, rational-choice perspectives from economics, and some learning theories from psychology are consistent with the basic idea of criminality. However, major portions of sociological labeling, strain, cultural, and conflict theories, those learning theories that emphasize the need to learn criminality and to enjoy crime, and those biological theories that suggest that "crime" is somehow directly inherited are strictly incompatible with the concept of criminality as we use it. Thus, although the perspective that we have outlined is fully multidisciplinary, it expresses a preference for some theories over others and makes no effort to integrate otherwise inconsistent points of view. The existence of competition preserves for this approach the possibility of falsification, a standard many integrated models are incapable of meeting.

### Implications for Crime Policy

Another advantage of the general theory is that it has concrete implications for public policy about crime. For example, it makes the traditional debate about focusing on offenders or offenses a directly testable or researchable issue (and it does so without prior commitment to one view rather than the other). Today, policymakers really do not know for any given "cause of delinquency" what the policy directives might be. In the real world causes of criminal acts do not come labeled as either propensities or opportunities. As a result, it is unclear to the policymaker whether intervention on the side of propensity or on the side of opportunity is indicated.

This theory allows causal variables to be sorted into those that affect the propensity to commit criminal acts and those that describe an environment conducive to such acts. For example, it should be possible to determine the extent to which family child-rearing practices affect the commission of criminal acts rather than the general criminality of the child. This is important to the extent that each dimension carries its own policy directives. In the former case (criminal acts), direct supervision of children neglected by their families should help to reduce crime. In the latter case (criminality), early intervention aimed at parent and child training would be indicated.

The theory can be illustrated further by its potential implications for education policy. Persons who oppose ability tracking suggest that such arrangements produce crime. Those who favor such arrangements argue that differences in criminal activity across ability groups stem from differences present before track assignments are made. A measure of criminality would allow the issue to be resolved. More important, the impact of differences in school organization or disciplinary practices can be directly assessed only when such individual tendencies are not confounded with school organization. For example, if large schools have more crime than small schools, we can ask whether this is due to differences in the criminality of the pupils, to differences in the "critical mass" of students with high crime potential, or to differences in the crime-control abilities of small and large schools. If large schools have more crime when their students do not differ in criminality, we can be reasonably confident that reducing school size would reduce the crime rate. At present this question cannot be resolved.

This conceptual scheme has implications for the traditional debate about the advisability of distinguishing between delinquents and "status offenders" in the juvenile justice system. Status offenses are, by definition, behaviors considered inappropriate for children that are, in some circumstances, acceptable for adults; incorrigibility, drug and alcohol use, truancy, and running away. Traditionally, the juvenile court assumed that such acts were early signs of a tendency to delinquency, evidence of danger of leading an immoral life. One purpose of the juvenile court was to intervene before these tendencies could manifest themselves in criminal acts, in purse snatching, rape, or robbery. Such a policy was seen to be in the best interests of the child and of society (because it saved both from a life of crime and punishment).

Recently, however, labeling and related social constructional theories have successfully challenged traditional juvenile court practices with the suggestion that status offenses are not indicative of a pattern or tendency and therefore do not justify such intervention. In fact, intervention is said to make matters worse, to increase the likelihood of subsequent criminal activity. Interestingly, there is now no generally accepted or reasonably articulated theory of delinquency sufficiently consistent with the traditional position of the juvenile court to provide the basis of a response to labeling views. The most prominent sociological views are either sympathetic to the labeling perspective (e.g. differential association, which shares with labeling theory the notion that the "definitions" of others are crucial in the causation of crime and criminality) or indifferent to it without being at the same time sympathetic to the role of the juvenile court, for example, integrated theory (Elliott et al., 1985), which explicitly assumes that delinquency requires peer support if it is to continue. Our theory suggests a resolution to this problem. If incorrigibility, being "beyond control," truancy, and early drug use are thought of as manifestations of an underlying tendency that is the same tendency underlying criminal acts, the interventionist tradition is correct. Our theory suggests that straightforward empirical resolution of this important public policy dispute is possible.

The general theory sheds new light on the deterrence question. It suggests that there is more than one way to achieve the "benefits" of crime, that some of these ways are legal, that the choice facing the offender is not necessarily among crimes but among pleasurable activities. As a consequence, the threat of sanctions may channel the offender's activity into equivalents of crime that are acceptable to society. To the extent this perspective is adequate, displacement may be an attractive goal of deterrence or of legal penalties rather than evidence of the limitation of such penalties. Put another way, the distinction between crime and criminality allows us to determine the extent to which sanctions have an effect when differences in criminality have been taken into account.

## Testing the Theory

The theory we have outlined here is, in our view, consistent with much data on crime (see Hirschi and Gottfredson, 1988). The theory is not, however, consistent with many currently popular perspectives. It asserts, for example, that criminality is contrary to pursuit of long-range goals, and is thus directly contrary to "strain" theory and to those economic theories that see crime as a career or occupation. Because our theory is directly contrary to strain theories, learning theories, and labeling theories, it is also incompatible with theories that subsume these perspectives (e.g. Wilson and Herrnstein, 1985).

Theories incompatible with other theories have the clear virtue of testability. The theory we propose makes problematic the contribution of crime and criminality factors to any given criminal event. This empirical uncertainty should not be confused with uncertainty about the importance of the distinction itself, or with uncertainty about the ways in which the theory differs from competing perspectives. These perspectives gloss over the distinction and in fact have no clear conception of their own dependent variable. The fact that they emphasize the illegality and "seriousness" of the offenses included in their measures of the dependent variable suggests that they are really interested in what we call crime. The fact that they conceptually restrict themselves to "sustained patterns of offending" or to "criminal careers" suggests that they are really concerned with what we call criminality. Unfortunately, none of the currently popular theories (with the possible exception of labeling theory), contains theoretical mechanisms capable of accounting for continuity of offending. The general conclusion must be, then, that competing theories are confused on the question of what it is they seek to explain, and that it is not difficult to find data where their predictions can be compared with those of a general theory of crime.

## Notes

1. This paper elaborates on earlier work in which we first encountered the need for the distinction between crime and criminality (Hirschi and Gottfredson, 1983), and on work that attempts to explore the conceptual (Hirschi and Gottfredson,

1988) and policy (Gottfredson and Hirschi, 1986) implications of the distinction.

## References

Buss, Arnold, and R. Plomin. 1975. *A Temperament Theory of Personality Development*. New York: Wiley.

Cohen, Albert K. 1955. *Delinquent Boys: The Culture of the Gang*. New York: Macmillan.

Cohen, Lawrence E., and M. Felson. 1979. "Social Change and Crime Rate Trends: A Routine Activities Approach." *American Sociological Review* 44:588-607.

Elliott, Delbert, David Huizinga, and Suzanne Ageton. 1985. *Explaining Delinquency and Drug Use*. Beverly Hills, Calif.: Sage Publications.

Glueck, Sheldon, and Eleanor Glueck. 1950. *Unraveling Juvenile Delinquency*. Cambridge, Mass.: Harvard University Press.

Gottfredson, Michael, and T. Hirschi. 1986. "The True Value of Lambda Would Appear to Be Zero: An Essay on Career Criminals, Criminal Careers, Selective Incapacitation, Cohort Studies, and Related Topics." *Criminology* 24:213-34.

Hindelang, Michael, M. Gottfredson, and J. Garofalo. 1978. *Victims of Personal Crime*. Cambridge, Mass.: Ballinger.

Hirschi, Travis, and M. Gottfredson. 1983. "Age and the Explanation of Crime." *American Journal of Sociology* 89:484-552.

_____. 1986. "The Distinction between Crime and Criminality." In *Critique and Explanation*, edited by T. Hartnagel and R. Silverman, pp. 55-69. New Brunswick, N.J.: Transaction Books.

_____. 1988. "Toward a General Theory of Crime." In *Understanding Crime: Interdisciplinary Perspectives*, edited by W. Buikhuisen and S. Mednick. Leiden: Brill.

McCord, Joan. 1979. "Some Child-rearing Antecedents of Criminal Behavior in Adult Men." *Journal of Personality and Social Psychology* 37:1477-86.

Mednick, Sarnoff. 1977. "A Bio-social Theory of the Learning of Law-abiding Behavior." In *Biosocial Bases of Criminal Behavior*, edited by S. Mednick and K. Christiansen. New York: Gardner.

Mednick, S., and K. Christiansen, eds. 1977. *Biosocial Bases of Criminal Behavior*. New York: Gardner.

Patterson, Gerald. 1980. "Children Who Steal." In *Understanding Crime*, edited by T. Hirschi and M. Gottfredson. Beverly Hills, Calif.: Sage Publications.

Schuessler, Karl, and D. Cressey. 1950. "Personality Characteristics of Criminals." *American Journal of Sociology* 55: 476-84.

West, Donald, and D. Farrington. 1977. *The Delinquent Way of Life*. London: Heinemann.

Wilson, James Q., and R. Herrnstein. 1985. *Crime and Human Nature*. New York: Simon & Schuster.

# 5

# An Interdisciplinary Theory of Criminal Behavior

## C. Ray Jeffery

### Criminology as an Interdisciplinary Science

Criminology had its origins in biology and psychology with such figures as Lombroso (medicine, biology), Freud (medicine, biology), and Pavlov (physiology, learning theory). Later on sociological theories were put forth by Durkheim, Sutherland, and others. As a result of these historical movements, criminology has developed a biological criminology and a sociological criminology, with little or no interaction among the several scientific disciplines.

At the same time the classical legal school of criminology emerged as an attempt to justify the use of punishment and the criminal justice system. Whereas the positive school of criminology was based on determinism, research as to the causes of behavior within the individual offender, and the treatment of criminal behavior by scientific means, the legalistic school was based on a concept of human nature derived from a mind-body dualism. Legalistic criminology held the offender responsible for his or her behavior according to the doctrine of free will and moral responsibility. The purpose of criminal law was to punish the offender according to some scale of pleasure and pain in order to deter criminal acts.

There exists today in criminology the need to bridge the gap between the scientific study of offenders and a criminal justice system that does not make use of criminology in its crime-control policies. Criminologists need (1) to integrate biological, psychological, and sociological theories of criminal behavior into an interdisciplinary theory of behavior, and (2) to integrate the scientific aspects of human behavior into criminal law and the criminal justice system. Crime control must shift from a just retribution and deterrence model to a prevention model based on preventing crime before it occurs (Jeffery, 1977).

I have been asked by the editors of this serial to develop a statement as to an interdisciplinary approach to criminal behavior. Although my training was in sociology, I have always identified with an interdisciplinary approach (Jeffery, 1979a), starting with criminal law and social philosophy, then psychology and learning theory, and more recently biology and brain functioning (Jeffery, 1979b; 1985; 1987). The most spectacular advancements in the past twenty years in the behavioral sciences have occurred in behavioral genetics, neurology, and neurochemistry, and it is my intent to discuss in a very brief fashion some of the implications of the newer interdisciplinary behavioral sciences for criminology with the hope of moving criminology into a more interdisciplinary framework.

Although my career has been devoted to an interdisciplinary approach, the approach is not unique with me. Wolfgang and Ferracuti (1967) argued for an integrated theory of behavior in *The Subculture of Violence*. They pointed out the eclecticism and pluralism of criminological theory, and the existing need for an integration of biology, psychology, and sociology into criminological research. Mueller (1969:199) has been a long-time advocate of the integration of criminal law and the behavioral sciences, and he has written that "a blind criminal justice, a deaf forensic psychiatry, and a dumb sociological criminology stand a good chance not only of survival— if they stand together—but of bettering humanity's plight."

## An Interdisciplinary Theory of Criminal Behavior

The theoretical model I am going to put forth in this article has been previously referred to as a "biosocial model" or a "bioenvironmental model" of criminal behavior. In a forthcoming book (Jeffery, 1989) I use the term "an interdisciplinary theory" of criminal behavior based on a systems approach to knowledge about human behavior. A systems approach places great emphasis on the interaction of biology, psychology, and sociology in the development of human behavior.

### The Nature of Human Nature

There are within Western philosophy two basic theories of human nature. Rationalism, as found in Plato, Descartes, and the rationalists, is based on a mind-body dualism in which a nonphysical entity (mind) controls a physical entity (body). The body is subject to the laws of nature and the laws of determinism; however, the mind is subject to its own laws and ways of analysis. The mind has the ability to reason and to know the nature of truth and reality. Ideas are innate to the individual, and independent of sensory experiences. Because the mind is independent of natural causation, it possesses free will and moral choice. The humanness of humankind is based on the fact that behavior is not determined but is free. Humankind can reflect on experiences and make decisions not based on biology, psychology, or sociology.

The other philosophical position is that of empiricism and positivism, as found in John Locke and the British empiricists. According to empiricism, the human being is born a *tabula rasa*, a blank tablet without ideas. Ideas come from sensory experiences and the association of these experiences into concepts and ideas. Such a view of life gives priority to the environment and the impact of the environment on human nature, in contrast to rationalism, which places such emphasis on the role of the individual in the creation of ideas and moral decisions.

Empiricism led to the scientific revolution and to the development of biology, psychology, and sociology, as well as physics and chemistry. Although the biologists, psychologists, and sociologists disagree as to the causes of behavior, they do agree that the natural laws of causation apply to human behavior because humankind is a part of nature.

The scientific view of behavior came into conflict with the philosophical view as found in rationalism and in the criminal law. Matson (1976) argues that the concept of humanistic beings (free moral agents) denies the existence of the human being as a machine beast (biological human beings, as found in Freud, Darwin, Lorenz, and Mendel) and the human being as a machine (Pavlov, Skinner, and modern psychology). The idea of the human being as a free moral agent is basic to criminal law, which is based on mental states (*mens rea*), free will, moral responsibility, and punishment for intentional wrongdoing. Criminological theory must be based on an integrated theory of behavior that can be applied to criminal law and to crime control models.

## Models of Behavior

Criminology is caught in the middle of philosophical and scientific controversies. One controversy involves the philosophical (free moral agent) versus scientific determinism argument. Another controversy involves mentalism versus physicalism. The mind-body dualism of Descartes created a nonphysical entity that controls the body. The monistic or holistic approach is based on physicalism and a unity of brain and body in an interdisciplinary system theory. There is further conflict between those who argue that the nature of human nature is determined at birth by biology and those who argue that human nature is determined by the environment and by experiences with the environment. This conflict involves the old heredity versus environment or nature versus nurture controversy.

Three schools of psychology can be identified as a result of these conflicts and controversies.

Model I:    Mentalism and Introspectionism
                Environment → Organism → Behavior
                            Mind

In Model I the environment enters the mind and is transformed into such mental states as concepts, attitudes, self-attitudes, values, and norms. These mental states in turn cause behavior. We never directly measure or observe the mental states, but we know that they exist because we infer them from behavior. Humanistic psychology, clinical psychology, and sociology use this model of behavior. Genetics, the brain, and biological variables are neglected or minimized.

                Model II:    Behaviorism
                Environment → Empty → Behavior
                            Organism

Behaviorism, as found in Watson and Skinner, is based on a stimulus-response model, or an environmental behavior model, Model II. The stimulus does not enter the brain or central nervous system, but acts directly on the response. No or little attention is paid to genetics and brain function in behaviorism because it is environmental determinism. This model of behavior is found in learning theory, behavioral theory, token economies, and behavioral modification programs.

Model III:    Interdisciplinary Theory of Behavior
                Environment → Organism → Behavior
                            Brain

In Model III organism and environment interact by means of the brain and central nervous system. This is a physical model of behavior as found in brain-body interaction. The brain is physical, it is directly measurable and observable, and it is not inferred from behavior. The environment influences behavior through the brain. This model of behavior is found in psychobiology, neurology, neurochemistry, biological psychiatry, and interdisciplinary criminology.

*The Nature of the Individual Organism*

The individual organism is essentially the product of three basic systems that involve three levels of analysis: genetics, brain structure and function, and learning theory. These three systems interact with one another and with the environment. This is an Organism x Environment (O x E) model of behavior, which can be diagrammed as follows:

Genetics ↔ Brain ↔ Behavior      (Learning/Personality)
                    ↝ Environment ↝

A brief discussion of each of these systems will be given to show how their interaction is basic to human behavior, including criminal behavior.

*Genetics and the Individual Organism* The individual organism is a product of genetics and the environment in interaction. The argument that human nature is either hereditary or environment has been replaced with the argument that human nature is a product of G x E = P (Phenotype), or genes and environment in interaction.

The genotype in interaction with the environment produces phenotype traits such as height, weight, skin color, body build, behavioral dispositions, and IQ. The controversial aspects of human genetics pertain to those related to behavior. No one denies that height or weight or skin color are genetically related, but many behavioral scientists are very uneasy about statements that IQ or violence or sex behavior are genetically related. Through twin studies, family studies, adoption studies, and experimental studies we know that there is a major genetic base for human behavior (Fuller and Thompson, 1978; Plomin, De Fries, and McClearn, 1980; Singer, 1985; Research and Education Association, 1982). The relationship between genetics and criminal behavior has been discussed in some detail in other places (Mednick and Volavka, 1980; Ellis, 1982; Rowe, 1986), and the general conclusion can be made that the link between genetics and criminal behavior has been established, but the real research in this area lies in the future.

It is important to emphasize for criminologists that this does not mean there is a gene for criminal behavior, or that there is a direct link between genes and behavior. Genes do not cause behavior, they cause phenotypic traits. The important traits or organs involved in behavior are those related to the brain, brain biochemistry, and the hormonal systems. The structure of the brain depends on the genetics x environment process, and in turn the type of brain the individual possesses determines the type of behavior the individual is capable of performing.

Through selective breeding geneticists have produced strains of fighting fish, or vicious dogs, or fast race horses, or superior types of corn. The same processes are at work in human genetics except we do not selectively breed human beings for violence or temperament. Most if not all of the theories of criminal behavior put forth in sociology, clinical psychology, and learning psychology totally ignore the genetic dimension of human nature and by doing so they miss half the process. They treat the human organism as an empty organism that is completely dominated by the environment to which it is exposed. As Konner (1982:80) has observed, "Any analysis of the causes of human nature that ignores either genes or the environment may safely be discarded."

*The Brain and Behavior* The organ of behavior is the brain, and the most important developments over the past twenty years in the behavioral sciences have to do with the development of such interdisciplinary fields as biological psychiatry, psychobiology, sociobiology, and neurological criminology (Kalat, 1984; Bloom, Lazerson, and Hofstadter, 1985; Thompson, 1985; Carlson, 1986). This is Model III, or the interdisciplinary mode of behavior.

The experiences the individual has with the environment must enter the body via the five senses and the sensory system. Sensory experiences are transformed into a biochemical code and transported to the brain. The brain has special areas for processing sensory information, such as the thalamus, the visual cortex, and the auditory cortex.

The brain processes, stores, and makes use of environmental input in order to control the motor system. The motor system consists of the cerebellum, the pyramidal system, and the extrapyramidal system. The motor system controls muscles and glands, or those processes we call behavior. If an arm moves, it is because a motor neuron has been activated. If a person commits a murder or rape or burglary, it is motor activity of the neurons. The immediate cause of behavior is motor neuron excitation or inhibition. The reason a group of motor neurons move an arm or leg is a very complex process involving millions of neurons, the past environmental history of the individual, the present physiological condition, and the past genetic history of the individual and the species.

Information is sent to the brain and received from the brain by two nervous systems known as the somatic nervous system and the autonomic nervous system. The somatic nervous system controls the large striated muscles that control the skeletal system, such as the arms and legs. What we refer to as "voluntary" behavior is under the control of the somatic nervous system because it is activated by a different part of the brain than is involuntary behavior.

The autonomic nervous system is controlled by the brain through the hypothalamus. The autonomic nervous system controls the internal organs of digestion, reproduction, and elimination as well as heart beat, blood pressure, and respiration rate. The activities of the autonomic nervous system are known as "involuntary" responses, for we do not usually think of ourselves as controlling our heart rate or digestion or blood pressure. This distinction between voluntary and involuntary movements is critical because the legal system makes a major distinction between voluntary and involuntary movements. Individuals are responsible only for voluntary movements. It is essential to understand the neurological bases for voluntary and involuntary movements, both of which are determined by the nervous system.

The autonomic nervous system is divided into sympathetic and parasympathetic. The sympathetic nervous system is an arousal system and it increases heart rate and blood pressure and respiration rate. This is the "fight-and-flight" response of the individual to danger. The sympathetic nervous system controls flight, fighting, food, and sexual behaviors.

The hypothalamus controls the pituitary gland, which in turn controls other glands, such as the adrenal glands over the kidneys. The adrenal glands produce epinephrine and norepinephrine, which in turn control the arousal response found in anger or aggression. The adrenal glands also produce steroid hormones related to sexual development and behavior, which in their turn influence the development of testosterone and estrogen by the testes and ovaries.

Another major center of the brain for emotional and motivational behavior is the limbic system in the midbrain. The limbic system is made up of parts of several different areas of the brain, including the hypothalamus, the thalamus, the mammillary bodies, and the septal nuclei, the amygdala, and the hippocampus. The limbic system is especially important in the case of anger, fear, and aggression. It is also involved in the control of hunger, sex, and thirst. The so-called pleasure centers of the brain are in the limbic system. The feeling of pleasure is related to the presence of the neurotransmitters norepinephrine and dopamine in the brain. Dopamine is also involved in the sensations of pleasure derived from the taking of cocaine and amphetamines.

The new brain, or the cerebral cortex, is the part of the brain controlling what we refer to as rationality, cognition, self-awareness, consciousness, thought, memory, learning, and language. It has sensory and motor areas, as well as a large associational area that connects sensory and motor activities. The ability of a human being to control the appetites and passions, and the ability to think and make decisions, to evaluate and make choices, and to plan for future contingencies belong to the cerebral cortex. Whether or not a person commits rape or murder or assault when confronted with a certain stimulus from the environment depends on the neural pathways from the cerebral cortex to the limbic system, and the ability of these pathways to control the neural activities of the limbic system that are related to violence and aggression.

*The Neurotransmitter System.* Neurons communicate with each other electrically and biochemically. The biochemical system is called the neurotransmitter system. Neurons do not join one another directly but are joined by a space called a synaptic cleft. Electrical activity in one neuron releases chemicals from the end of the axon into the synaptic cleft, where these chemicals stimulate the receptor neurons on the next neuron. Because all behavior depends on neural activity, and neural activity is biochemical activity, the neurotransmitters are critical to our behavior and to our understanding of our behavior.

The major neurotransmitters are

- Epinephrine (adrenaline)
- Norepinephrine (noradrenaline)
- Dopamine
- Serotonin
- Acetylcholine
- GABA

An important link between the environment and behavior is diet because food intake has a profound influence on the neurotransmitters. Acetylcholine is synthesized from choline, which is found in eggs, liver, and butter, among other foods. Serotonin is a product of tryptophan, an amino acid that is derived from food products. Tyrosine, found in food also, is a precursor to dopamine, epinephrine, and norepinephrine.

*The Neurotransmitter System and Abnormal Behavior.* The neurotransmitters have been involved in the behaviors usually classified as mental illness or criminal. Schizophrenia is related to high levels of dopamine, and depression to low levels of norepinephrine. Violent behavior is related to low levels of serotonin. This suggests that one possible means for controlling violence is through higher levels of tryptophan in the diets of those predisposed to violence (Lieberman and Wurtman, 1986).

Behavioral disorders are now being treated with drugs, the major categories being (a) the antidepression drugs, (b) the antianxiety drugs, (c) the antipsychotic drugs, and (d) lithium. The new biological psychiatry has joined psychiatry, psychopharmacology, and neurology in a major interdisciplinary effort to understand human behavior (Carlton, 1983; Lickey and Gordon, 1983; Snyder, 1980; Pincus and Tucker, 1985; Andreasen, 1984).

*The Brain and Criminal Behavior.* The brain is an information-processing system that uses biochemical codes. Anything that interferes with this processing system causes behavioral disturbances because the brain controls behavior. Such interference can come from brain trauma and head injuries; diet and nutrition; metabolic disorders; exposure to drugs, alcohol, lead, and cadmium; epilepsy; blood vessel disorders; and degenerative disorders (Roberts, 1984; Pincus and Tucker, 1985). Lewis et al. (1986)

examined fifteen death row inmates and found that all had a history of severe head injuries, seven had major neurological impairments, and others had shown signs of neurological disorders. Yeudall (1977) found brain damage and brain dysfunction in 91 percent of the psychopaths he examined in the Alberta Hospital, and many of these suffered from left-hemisphere dysfunction. Hypoglycemia has often been associated with antisocial behaviors in children and adults (Virkunen, 1986). An assessment of these studies (Harper and Gans, 1986) concluded that many of them could be faulted for methodological reasons, but in general a complex interaction occurs between diet and behavior that is influenced by genetics and environment. Appropriate biochemical tests, such as glucose-tolerance tests and blood-hormone-level tests, are needed. Each individual reacts to diet, including sugar intake, in a different way.

As noted, low serotonin levels in the brain are related to violence; the food supplement tryptophan is a precursor to serotonin and can be used to increase the serotonin levels in the brain. Diets rich in carbohydrates increase the tryptophan levels in the brain, whereas diets rich in proteins decrease the tryptophan levels (Lieberman and Wurtman, 1986; Wurtman, 1986).

The limbic system of the brain is the center for violence and aggression. Damage to this area can cause epileptic seizures, episodic violence, learning disorders, and other brain dysfunctions. The limbic system is very responsive to the neurotransmitters, especially to serotonin and testosterone levels (Valzelli, 1981; Carlson, 1986).

A model of behavior control can be derived from the organization of the brain. Violence is a product of the limbic system, whereas the control of violence is by the cerebral cortex.

*Learning.* Except for simple reflex actions, higher primate behavior is learned behavior. Learning is the modification of behavior by experience (Schwartz, 1978; Fantino and Logan, 1979; Bower and Hilgard, 1981; Domjan and Burkhard, 1982). Psychologists and sociologists regard learning as a denial of genetics and brain activity, but to say that learning occurs is not to deny biology or the biological foundations of behavior. Rats can be bred to be dull or bright, and all learning takes place in the brain.

Learning involves a stimulus (environment) exciting a neuronal system in the brain, which then activates motor neurons (behavior). This is referred to in learning theory as a stimulus-response relationship. If the stimulus produces a response without prior experience or learning the relationship is referred to as an unconditional stimulus (US)-unconditional response (UR) relationship. Food (US) will produce salivation (UR) because of the manner in which the brain is wired. The stimulus food activates the autonomic nervous system, which in term activates the salivary gland. Ivan Pavlov discovered that when a bell was sounded before presentation of food, the experimental animal (dogs in this instance) would learn to salivate at the sound of the bell without the presence of food. The dog learned to associate the bell, called a conditioned stimulus (CS), with food (US). The association of the CS with the US is associational learning.

Pavlovian conditioning is called classical learning theory. American learning theory is called operant learning theory as developed by Watson, Skinner, and others. Operant conditioning involves the organism's responding to the environment in order to receive a stimulus. This is R-S learning, or Response-Stimulus learning. If the stimulus increases a response rate, it is labeled reinforcement; if the stimulus decreases the response rate, it is called punishment.

Operant learning theory totally denies the concept of a "mind," and it also denies the roles of genetics or the brain in behavior. It ignores the biological changes that occur in the brain as a result of environmental experiences. It is an empty organism theory, or a S-R theory or model II, as opposed to an S-O-R, or stimulus-organism response model which places emphasis on the nature of the organism. Operant learning is totally environmental in its interpretation of learned behavior.

Modern learning theory is based on neurology because the brain is the organ of learning, and neurons and neural transmitters are modified as a result of learning (Kalat, 1984; Carlson, 1986). Domjan and Burkhard (1982:12) state that "learning is an enduring change in the neural mechanism of behavior that results from experience with the environment." Bower and Hilgard (1981:475) note that "nothing is more certain than that our behavior is a product of our nervous system."

Although criminological theories of behavior place emphasis on learning, they do not make use of or acknowledge the existence of psychology or psychological learning theories. With the exception of social learning theory based on the idea of imitation, sociologists have not developed learning theory. Jeffery (1965) attempted to reinterpret learning theory in terms of Skinnerian theory, but this effort was generally ignored in order to remain with differential association as discussed in Sutherland (Jeffery, 1977).

An integrated theory of criminal behavior must include a statement as to the ways in which pain and pleasure are related to the pleasure and pain centers of the brain and to operant conditioning and reinforcement. Punishment is a major aspect of learning theory as well as criminology, and the principles of learning as they apply to punishment must be utilized by criminologists in their discussions of punishment, deterrence, and the criminal justice system.

Social variables such as social class, status, and reputation become conditioned stimuli or conditioned reinforcers because of their association with primary or unconditioned stimuli. The relationship of learned behavior, especially social learning, to biology and the brain must be spelled out in criminological theories.

## Sociological Theories of Criminal Behavior

Sociological theories can be divided into microtheories and macrotheories, or theories dealing with the individual person and theories dealing with groups, social structure, and subcultures. Sociology has been described as a multiple-paradigm science (Ritzer, 1975; Ritzer, 1983), and as a science of two sociologies, sociological and individualistic (Wentworth, 1980). Dawe (1978) argues that social action theory (action of individual actors) is the heart of sociology, and he reduces social systems theory to social action theory.

Ritzer (1975, 1983; see also Coser, 1977; Turner, 1982) classified sociological theory into (1) social factism or social structuralism, including structure-functionalism and conflict theory; (2) social definitionism, or psychological sociology, including symbolic interactionism, phenomenology, ethnomethodology, and existentialism; and (3) social behaviorism or Skinnerian psychology applied to social behavior, as found in exchange theory and behavioral sociology.

Sociological theories are marked by two basic assumptions. (1) From Durkheim, the sociologist derived his or her view that behavior is strictly social and that biological and psychological levels of analysis are to be ignored. Social facts are real, and these social facts are external to the individual and coercive on the individual (Ritzer, 1983:15). (2) Human nature is a combination of a Cartesian dualism of mind and body and a Lockean *tabula rasa* or empty-organism view of human nature. Humankind is born devoid of biological and psychological nature and propensities, and what an individual becomes is a result of socialization through contact with other human beings and with cultural norms and values. The individual's genetic history or brain structure in no way enters into his or her responses to environmental pressures. The social environment is not processed through the brain according to sociological theories, but somehow the social environment is transformed into mental states called self-concepts, attitudes, values, and norms. Shoemaker in his *Theories of Delinquency* states the problem in this way: "Even if sociologists provide evidence that environmental factors offer the best explanations for delinquency, they would still eventually be forced to account for the translation of these influences into behavior, whether this occurs through reasoning abilities, subconscious motives, or personality characteristics" (1984:65). Several sociologists have responded to the sociological view of nature that is based on social environmentalism and mentalism. Wrong (1961) in his article on the oversocialized concept of the human being notes that sociologists ignore the fact that in "the beginning there is the body." Wolfgang and Ferracuti (1967) point to the need for an interdisciplinary approach to criminology, including psychology, and they cite several sociologists who want to include biology and psychology in sociological theories. Inkeles (1959) wrote that sociology needs psychology, and he is critical of Durkheim's famous study of suicide, which was based on a society-rate-of-suicide model. In its place Inkeles would use a society-personality-rate-of-behavior model, a model that uses psychology as an interesting variable or level of analysis between the environment and behavior. Gove and Carpenter (1982) comment on the sterility of sociological theory and they note that "the idea that the human mind and body are separate entities is no longer a tenable position." They cite a number of sociologists who criticize the field for not advancing, for being overmethodological and statistical, and for being epistemological. Van den Berghe (1974, 1975) argued that sociology must "bring beasts back into sociology," and Homans (1964) in his presidential address to the American Sociological Association argued that sociologists must "bring man back into sociology." Homans has used Skinnerian psychology as a basis for sociological analysis, for which he has been labeled a "psychological reductionist" (Ritzer, 1983). The seeds have been planted for an integration of biology, psychology, and sociology by the individuals cited above, but the integration and development of such a theory of human behavior is still to come.

Sociological theories of criminal behavior follow the basic assumptions of sociological theories in general. Some deal with the social structure, borrowing from Durkheim, Parsons, and Merton, as found in the works of Cloward and Ohlin, and Cohen. Crime is caused by social structure and not by individual traits. Means and ends or social-class values are not integrated, and criminal behavior is a result of learning or not learning certain norms and certain values. Following Durkheim's view of social structure, sociologists assume that individuals are constrained by social norms, but they do not show us how social norms get inside the individual or how they control behavior. Merton (1957:131-32) stated that the causes of delinquency and social deviance lie in the social structure and not in the individual. Cohen (1959:462) echoed this sentiment when he noted that theories of criminality should be sociological and not psychological, and he was critical of Sutherland and his theory of differential association for being so psychological.

Sociological theories that deal with the individual level of analysis focus on socialization patterns and how individuals are caught in subcultural normative conflicts. Sutherland's theory of differential association is a model of the subcultural approach. It's a social learning theory and totally ignores biological and psychological aspects of learning. As Schuessler (Sutherland, 1974) stated in the introduction to Sutherland's book, "He [Sutherland] was consistently sociological in his analysis of crime and did not broaden his theoretical model to accommodate biological and psychological factors" (p. ix).Sutherland did not understand learning theory, and in fact, he misconstrued learning theory (Kornhauser, 1978:196-97). Jeffery (1965) attempted to reformulate Sutherland's theory in terms of Skinnerian learning theory, but this effort was ignored when Burgess and Akers (1966) wrote that Sutherland's theory could be restated as differential social reinforcement and thus left in sociology. Akers has consistently argued that criminal behavior involves social and not psychological learning theory, and that the rewards for crime are social and not psychological, biological, and/or material (Akers, 1977; Akers, 1981; Gibbons and Krohn, 1986). Whereas Cohen argued that Sutherland was too psychological in his theory of learning, Akers (1981) argued that Sutherland's theory of learning must be placed in sociology, not psychology. Is Sutherland's theory sociological, psychological, or social psychological? These sorts of issues occur when we lack an integrated theory of behavior and we assume behavior is either biological or psychological or sociological rather than an interaction of all three.

The major issue in sociological theories is the lack of attention to the individual offender, and the related issue of how the environment gets into the organism if there is no brain and no physical structure. The sociologist uses inferred mental states taken from symbolic interactionism, phenomenology, and ethnomethodology to explain human behavior. Coser (1975) in his presidential address to the American Sociological Association noted that sociology lacked a theoretical base, was caught in an overemphasis on methodology, and was engaged in an orgy of subjectivism as the sociologist tried to find out what was going on in the mind of the social actor (Coser, 1975:698; Ritzer, 1983:287). Coser proposed that macrosociology or social structure is the real subject matter of sociology. The inability of the sociologist to define his or her subject matter or to come up with a biopsychological theory of human behavior upon which to base this theoretical structure has greatly handicapped the development of sociological criminology.

Ritzer (1983:311), in his classification of social theories, classified macro social factism as macro objective and macro subjective, whereas social definitionism is micro subjective. The only paradigm that is micro objective with physical objects as referents is social behaviorism taken from Skinner and his denial of mentalistic concepts. This theory (Jeffery, 1965) has never been popular in criminology because it runs counter to the mentalism and subjectivism and voluntarism of U.S. sociology. As Ritzer (1983:310) has noted, a great many sociological phenomena are in the realm of ideas without material existence, such as the social construction of reality, norms, values and culture.

## Biology and Sociology: An Integration

The real need now is to integrate biochemistry, neurology, psycho-biology, and learning theory with such sociological concepts as social class, race, sex, and age. Several examples will be given as to how this might be done, but this is not intended as a major discussion of these issues.

Males commit more crimes than females. Males differ from females in terms of XX-XY chromosomes, in terms of brain structure, and in terms of hormonal systems. Sex is a biological, psychological, and sociological variable, and it must be viewed in terms of the interaction of the brain on several different levels of analysis. The impact of sex on brain organization, and the impact of brain organization on sexual behavior, violence, and aggression are topics of interest to sociologists that must be explored in criminology (Gove and Carpenter, 1982:117ff.,137ff.). We need a better linkage of age and sex to crime through biological and psychological inter-vening variables. To the sociologist, sex means the social experiences en-countered in a social environment, and not the physical organism and the biological foundations of sexual differences.

Another relationship between biology and sociology that should be ex-plored is that between environmental pollution and the brain. The brain is a biochemical system, and it is very sensitive to pollutants such as lead and cadmium; when the brain is polluted, behavior is corrupted. It is known that pollution can destroy brain cells, and it is also known that the lower classes are more often subjected to this pollution. Another link between the brain and environment is that of diet and nutrition. What we eat is trans-formed into biochemicals for the brain, and these biochemicals in turn influence behavior. Minimal brain damage and learning disabilities are related to antisocial behaviors. We know that different social classes have different diets and different crime rates. The link between social class and crime, or poverty and crime, may be the brain because whatever occurs in the environment alters the brain and thereby behavior. Poverty involves a certain type of diet and exposure to certain heavy metals and other pollu-tants which then enter the brain. Poverty alters the brain, which then controls behavior.

Another way in which biology and sociology can be integrated is in terms of conflict theory or Marxian theory. The idea of conflict is basic to biology and evolutionary theory. The principal conflicts occur at the inter-species level, as the destruction of one species by another species in a predator-prey relationship, e.g. the destruction of many species on earth by humankind. Another level of conflict is intraspecies conflict between males for dominance over territory and females, for purposes of mating and food supply. Even at the human level male-male aggression and dominance is a major and critical feature of social and psychological life. Another level of human conflict and competition is between individuals, both male and female, for the basic essentials for survival. Even within the individual there is great conflict between biological needs, as found in the limbic system, and psychological and social needs, as found in socialization, learning, and the cerebral cortex. Each individual must control his or her basic urges and needs every moment of every day. By limiting the analysis of conflict to social classes and power relationships, the conflict theorist ignores or minimizes the fact that other levels of conflict are occurring that are much more critical than social-class conflict. Any adult male is so concerned each day with his sexual needs, his need for food, his need for a job, his need for social status and recognition, and his need for physical security and safety that he has little if any time to be concerned about participating in social class conflict.

## What Is Interdisciplinary Criminology?

When we speak of an interdisciplinary approach to crime and criminal behavior, we must be careful to make it clear what we mean. We do not mean a multidisciplinary approach wherein a little genetics, a little personality theory, a little learning theory, and a little psychobiology is presented. This is the usual way in which textbooks that try to introduce biology and psychology into criminology handle these issues (see Fox, 1985; Siegal, 1986; Gibbons, 1982; Shoemaker, 1984). Topics are introduced, statements are made about the lack of a total theory in psychology and biology, and then the authors go on to discuss sociological theories without any reference to the biological and psychological foundations of sociological concepts.

A truly interdisciplinary approach integrates the levels of analysis. Genetics is discussed as it pertains to the development of the brain and learning and of behavioral systems. The brain is discussed as it relates to learning, to violence and aggression, to sexual behaviors, to pleasure and pain, to mental illness, and to cultural adaptations to the environment. Learning theory is discussed as it relates to genetics, to the brain, to cultural adaptation, to violence and aggression, to sexual behavior, to mental illness, and to antisocial behaviors. Social and cultural variables are discussed as they influence and are influenced by genetics, the brain, learning processes, and personality development. Genes influence societies and societies influence genes.

## Why Some Do, Some Do Not

A major question in sociology has always been, "Why some do and some don't." Some of the poor are criminals and some are not. Some females are criminals, and some are not. Some urban dwellers are criminals, and some are not. Shoemaker (1984:175-76) states that control theory is the best sociological theory but even it fails to explain all acts of delinquency, and it fails to predict specific acts of delinquency.

Social control theory as presented by Hirschi (1969) stands in opposition to social strain and cultural deviance theories. Strain and deviance theories assume conformity to social norms and then attempt to explain deviance. If a person desires to obey social norms, why then is he or she a deviant? (Hirschi, 1969:5). The sociologist cannot explain deviance if he or she assumes that people as social animals are conformist to norms, so he or she resorts to strain and cultural conflict theories. As Hirschi notes, control theory starts by assuming that humankind is deviant and that conformity is imposed on it by social bonding. He cites Hobbes and the notion that in nature life is "brutish, nasty, and short."

This again raises the question of the nature of human nature. If humankind is by nature antisocial, as Freud, Hobbes, and others have argued, then a theory of criminal behavior must start with a theory of human nature based on biological and psychological elements that oppose those of the social system. This is what Freud did, and this is basically the argument in my interdisciplinary approach to behavior. The human being starts with basic biological and psychological needs and urges that are in direct conflict with those of other human beings. In order to exist as a society, human beings must create expensive and powerful controls over human nature, as found in the state system and in criminal law. From the sociological perspective (except for social control theory), the human being is born without a human nature and is socialized into conformity. A lack of conformity means a lack of proper socialization or socialization into the wrong value system. From the point of view of control theory and interdisciplinary theory, the human being is born with a biological and psychological nature quite independent of the socialization process of the environment; a brain and hormones makes the human being violent and sexually aggressive. Society does not cause sex and violence, but it tries to respond to these behaviors with social control mechanisms.

The basic answers to the issues raised are quite simple. No two people are alike. Social pressures on individuals result in quite different behaviors in different people. Why do some poor people commit crimes and other poor people do not? We will never know if we study only groups on the basis of aggregate data. However, if we look at poor people as individuals, we will discover that each person has a different genetic system, a different brain, a different pattern of learned responses, and a different set of experiences with the environment.

Why is it that we cannot predict individual criminal activity? Again, to predict individual acts we must study individuals. To predict which person out of a hundred will be violent in the next ten years, we must know as much as possible about each of the hundred from as many perspectives as possible. We will never be able to predict human behavior from group data. Groups do not commit crimes, only individuals do.

Shoemaker (1984:176) states that the immediate precursors to criminal behavior are social bonds and self-concept. These exist in the social environment and must be internalized if social control is to take place. According to interdisciplinary theory, the immediate precursors of behavior are neurons in action in the brain. Every time a muscle moves it is because of the brain. No muscle has ever been moved by a social bond or a self-concept.

## References

Akers, R.L. 1977. *Deviant Behavior: A Social Learning Approach.* 2d ed. Belmont, Calif.: Wadsworth.

_____. 1981. "Reflections of a Social Behaviorist on Behavioral Sociology." *American Sociologist* 16: 177-80.

Andreasen, N.C. 1984. *The Broken Brain: The Biological Revolution in Psychiatry.* New York: Harper & Row.

Bloom, F.E., A. Lazerson, and L. Hofstadter. 1985. *Brain, Mind, and Behavior.* New York: Freeman.

Bower, G.H., and E.R. Hilgard. 1981. *Theories of Learning.* Englewood Cliffs, N.J.: Prentice-Hall.

Burgess, R.L., and R.L. Akers. 1966. "A Differential Association-Reinforcement Theory of Criminal Behavior." *Social Problems* 14 (Fall):128-47.

Carlson, N.E. 1986. *Physiology of Behavior.* Boston: Allyn & Bacon.

Carlton, P.L. 1983. *A Primer of Behavior Pharmacology.* New York: Freeman.

Cohen, A.K. 1959. "The Study of Social Disorganization and Deviant Behavior." In *Sociology Today*, edited by R.K. Merton, L. Broom, and L.S. Cottrell, Jr. New York: Basic Books.

Coser, L. 1977. *Masters in Sociological Thought.* New York: Harcourt Brace Jovanovich.

_____. 1975. "Two Methods in Search of a Substance." *American Sociological Review* 40:691-700.

Dawe, A. 1978. "Theories of Social Action." In *A History of Sociological Analysis*, edited by T. Bottomore and R. Nisbet. New York: Basic Books.

Domjan, M., and B. Burkhard. 1982. *The Principles of Learning and Behavior.* Belmont, Calif.: Brooks/Cole.

Ellis, L. 1982. "Genetics and Criminal Behaviors." *Criminology* 20: 43-66.

Fantino, E., and C. A. Logan. 1979. *The Experimental Analysis of Behavior.* San Francisco: Freeman.

Fox, V. 1985. *Introduction to Criminology.* Englewood Cliffs, N.J.: Prentice-Hall.

Fuller, J.L., and W.R. Thompson. 1978. *Foundations of Behavioral Genetics.* St. Louis: Mosby.

Gibbons, D.C. 1982. *Society, Crime and Criminal Behavior.* 4th ed. Englewood Cliffs, N.J.: Prentice-Hall.

Gibbons, D.C., and M.D. Krohn. 1986. *Delinquent Behavior.* 4th ed. Englewood Cliffs, N.J.: Prentice-Hall.

Gove, W.R., and G.R. Carpenter. 1982. *The Fundamental Connection between Nature and Nurture.* Lexington, Mass.: Heath.

Harper, A.E., and D.A. Gans. 1986. "Carbohydrate Intake and Children's Behavior." *Overview* (January):142-50.

Hirschi, T. 1969. *Causes of Delinquency.* Berkeley: University of California Press.

Homans, G.C. 1964. "Bringing Men Back In." *American Sociological Review* 29:809-18.

Inkeles, A. 1959. "Personality and Social Structure." In *Sociology Today,* edited by R.K. Merton, L. Broom, and L.S. Cottrell, Jr. New York: Basic Books.

Jeffery, C.R. 1965. "Criminal Behavior and Learning Theory." *Journal of Criminal Law, Criminology, and Police Science* 56 (September): 294-300.

————. 1977. *Crime Prevention through Environmental Design.* Beverly Hills, Calif.: Sage Publications.

————. 1979a. "Criminology as an Interdisciplinary Behavioral Science." In *Criminology: New Concerns,* edited by E. Sagarin. Beverly Hills, Calif.: Sage Publications.

————. 1979b. *Biology and Crime.* Beverly Hills, Calif.: Sage Publications.

————. 1985. *Attacks on the Insanity Defense: Biological Psychiatry and New Perspectives on Criminal Behavior.* Springfield, Ill.: Charles C Thomas.

————. 1987. "Criminal Law, Biological Psychiatry, and Premenstrual Syndrome: Conflicting Perspectives." In *Premenstrual Syndrome,* edited by B.E. Ginsburg and B.F. Carter. New York: Plenum.

————. 1989. *Criminology: An Interdisciplinary Approach.* Englewood Cliffs, N.J.: Prentice-Hall.

Kalat, J.W. 1984. *Biological Psychology.* Belmont, Calif.: Wadsworth.

Konner, Melvin. *The Tangled Wing: Biological Constraints on the Human Spirit.* New York: Holt, Rinehart, and Winston, 1982.

Kornhauser, R.R. 1978. *Social Sources of Delinquency.* Chicago: University of Chicago Press.

Lewis, D.O., et al. 1986. "Psychiatric, Neurological, and Psycho-Educational Characteristics of 15 Death Row Inmates in the United States." *American Journal of Psychiatry* 143: 838-45.

Lickey, M.E., and B. Gordon. 1983. *Drugs for Mental Illness.* New York: Freeman.

Lieberman, H.R., and R.J. Wurtman. 1986. "Foods and Food Constituents That Affect the Brain and Human Behavior." *Overview* (January):139-41.

Matson, F.W. 1976. *The Idea of Man.* New York: Delta.

Mednick, S.A., and J. Voluvka. 1980. "Biology and Crime." In *Crime and Justice,* edited by N. Morris and M. Tonry. Chicago: University of Chicago Press.

Merton, R.K. 1957. "Social Structure and Anomie." In *Social Theory and Social Structure*, by R.K. Merton. New York: Free Press.

Mueller, G.O.W. 1969. *Crime and the Scholars*. Seattle: University of Washington Press.

Pincus, J.M., and G.J. Tucker. 1985. *Behavioral Neurology*. New York: Oxford University Press.

Plomin, R., J.C. De Fries, and G.E. McClearn. 1980. *Behavioral Genetics: A Primer*. San Francisco: Freeman.

Research and Education Association. 1982. *Behavioral Genetics*. New York: Research and Education Association.

Ritzer, G. 1983. *Contemporary Sociological Theory*. New York: Knopf.

_____. 1975. *Sociology: A Multiple Paradigm Science*. Boston: Allyn & Bacon.

Roberts, J.K.A. 1984. *Differential Diagnosis in Neuropsychiatry*. New York: Wiley.

Rowe, D.C. 1986. "Genetic and Environmental Components of Antisocial Behavior: A Study of 165 Twin Pairs." *Criminology* 24:3 (August):513-42.

Schwartz, B. 1978. *Psychology of Learning and Behavior*. New York: Norton.

Shoemaker, D.J. 1984. *Theories of Delinquency*. New York: Oxford University Press.

Siegel, L.J. 1986. *Criminology*. 2d ed. St. Paul, Minn.: West.

Singer, S. 1985. *Human Genetics*. New York: Freeman.

Snyder, S.H. 1980. *Biological Aspects of Mental Disorder*. New York: Oxford University Press.

Sutherland, E.H. 1974. *Edwin H. Sutherland: On Analyzing Crime*. Chicago: University of Chicago Press.

Thompson, R.F. 1985. *The Brain*. New York: Freeman.

Turner, J.H. 1982. *The Structure of Sociological Theory*. Homewood, Ill.: Dorsey Press.

Valzelli, L. 1981. *Psychobiology of Violence and Aggression*. New York: Raven Press.

Van den Berghe, P. 1974. "Bringing Beasts Back In: Toward Biosocial Theory of Aggression." *American Sociological Review* 39:3, 777-88.

_____. 1975. *Man in Society: A Biosocial View*. New York: Elsevier.

Virkunen, M. 1986. "Insulin Secretion during the Glucose Tolerance Test among Habitually Violent and Impulsive Offenders." *Aggressive Behavior* 12:303-10.

Wentworth, W. 1980. *Context and Understanding: An Inquiry into Socialization Theory*. New York: Elsevier.

Wolfgang, M.E., and F. Ferracuti. 1967. *The Subculture of Violence*. London: Tavistock.

Wrong, D. 1961. "The Oversocialized Conception of Man." *American Sociological Review* 26:183-92.

Wurtman, J. 1986. *Managing Your Mind and Mood through Food*. New York: Rawson Associates.

Yeudall, L.T. 1977. "Neuropsychological Assessment of Forensic Disorders." *Canada's Mental Health* 25: 7-16.

# 6

# Personality and Criminality: A Dispositional Analysis

*Hans J. Eysenck*

There are fashions in scientific theories just as there are in feminine apparel, and theories of criminality are no exception. In the nineteenth century psychological theories of criminality implicating genetic causes and personality features characteristic of criminals were widely accepted, finally giving rise to the theory of "Il Reo Nato" (the born criminal) of Lombroso. Since then fashion has swung round to favor sociological theories, i.e. theories implicating social causes like poverty, inequality, bad housing, and so on. These theories have been widely accepted in spite of two grave faults. In the first place, it is clear that social causes can act only through individual persons; in other words, psychological causes are still predominant. Poverty, inequality, and bad housing cannot by themselves produce any effects; it is only the psychological reactions of human beings to these social factors that may or may not produce criminal behavior.

The other fault is even more telling. If poverty, inequality, and bad housing are the causes of crime, then any improvement in these conditions should lead to a diminution of criminality. In actual fact the correlation is positive rather than negative. Over the past fifty years there has been a tremendous improvement in the material conditions of people in the capitalist countries, inequality has decisively diminished, and physical conditions such as housing and the like have improved. Yet, there has been a tremendous increase in crime. It is very difficult to see how sociological theories can cope with this reversal of the predicted relationship.

Concurrent with the apparent failure of sociological theories has been an increase in research into personality correlates of criminality, suggesting that genetic factors, personality features, and temperament variables do

89

play a very important part in the genesis of antisocial conduct. This research has given rise to causal theories, such as those of Eysenck (1977), which have received a good deal of support. These theories are closely linked with personality, and in this chapter we will review briefly some of the literature that suggests that the rejection of psychological causes in criminality may have been premature.

It is impossible to review the whole literature, hence we will confine ourselves to studies relevant to Eysenck's theory implicating three major dimensions of personality: psychoticism, extraversion, and neuroticism (Eysenck and Eysenck, 1985). These major dimensions of personality are derived from detailed statistical analysis of intercorrelations between traits, demonstrating that in the great majority of published studies of trait intercorrelations in different populations, in different countries, and using different inventories, these three major factors are found again and again. To make the discussion more readily intelligible, figures 1, 2, and 3 show the trait whose intercorrelations give rise to the postulation of the dimensions of psychoticism (P), extraversion (E), and neuroticism (N).

These three major dimensions of personality are not selected on an arbitrary basis; they share certain characteristics that single them out from many other suggested primary personality variables. (1) As Royce and Powell (1983) have shown, it is these three dimensions that emerge again and again from multivariate analyses of personality. (2) The dimensions are universal, and not confined to Western culture (Eysenck and Barratt, 1985). (3) The dimensions have a strong genetic basis, which accounts for between one-half and two-thirds of the total variance (Eysenck and Eysenck, 1985). (4) The dimensions have a strong basis in physiological features of the central and autonomic nervous systems (Eysenck and Eysenck, 1985). (5) The dimensions are closely linked with social behavior, such as sexual behavior, neurotic behavior, and criminality (Eysenck, 1981).

Predictions based on Eysenck's (1977) theory are that criminality would be correlated with a high degree of psychoticism, a high degree of neuroticism, and a high degree of extraversion. This prediction is qualified to some extent by the addition that criminality is not entirely homogeneous, so that different types of crime may be correlated differently with these personality features, and by another proviso that age is relevant to the observed correlations, in the sense that for younger boys and girls extraversion would be more important than neuroticism, whereas for adult criminals neuroticism would be more important than extraversion (Eysenck and Gudjonsson, in press). Psychoticism is believed to be correlated with criminality at all stages.

Passingham (1972) has reviewed earlier work relevant to this theory, with indifferent results. There are many reasons for this. Many studies were not

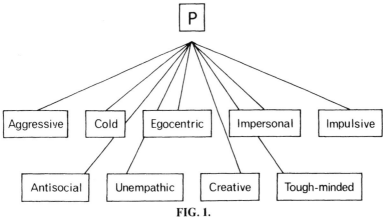

**FIG. 1.**
**Traits defining Psychoticism.**

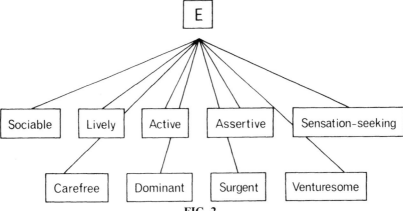

**FIG. 2.**
**Traits defining Extraversion.**

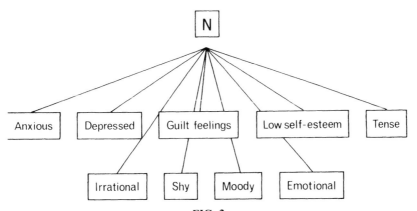

**FIG. 3.**
**Traits defining Neuroticism.**

planned or carried out to test the theories specifically, and are of doubtful relevance. There was often failure to control for dissimulation through the use of lie scales. The fact that criminals are not a homogeneous group was disregarded; different investigators have studied different populations specializing in different types of crime. Age was not taken into account. Other problems are considered by Eysenck (1977). It would seem better to confine attention to later studies, geared to the theory in question, and using inventories directly relevant, such as the EPI and the EPQ. Such a review of later studies is presented by Eysenck (1977) with much more positive results.

In spite of the heterogeneity undoubtedly present in prison populations, it can be shown that there is some generality also. Thus, Table 1 (Eysenck, 1977) shows the result of what is probably the largest investigation comparing prisoners and suitable controls (male). There are altogether 1,870 prisoners, and 1,987 controls, in two independent studies carried out by S.B.G. Eysenck and A. McLean, respectively. It will be seen that in both investigations prisoners are very significantly higher on P, E, and N, as demanded by the theory. Such a result cannot be invalidated by the usual small-scale studies of groups of a hundred or fewer prisoners and controls, tested under unspecified motivational conditions, often with unsuitable instruments, and not controlled for such variables as age. Yet this is precisely what meta-analysis would do.

The design of the study just mentioned is a classical one in which a group of convicted offenders, usually incarcerated, is compared with a control group, equated on a number of variables such as age, social status, sex, and so on, with respect to personality variables of one kind or another. Such a design, while informative, has one obvious disadvantage in that the control group will almost undoubtedly contain a number of people who should be counted as "criminals," except for the fact that they have not been caught! In other words, assuming as we do a continuum of antisocial

### TABLE 1
P, E, and N scores of groups of adult male prisoners and controls: data from two independent investigations from Eysenck.

| | n | Psychoticism | Extraversion | Neuroticism |
|---|---|---|---|---|
| S.B.G. Eysenck | | | | |
| (a) Prisoners | 1301 | $6.55 \pm 3.16$ | $12.51 \pm 3.63$ | $11.39 \pm 4.97$ |
| (b) Controls | 1392 | $4.10 \pm 2.53$ | $11.65 \pm 4.37$ | $9.73 \pm 4.71$ |
| | | $P < 0.001$ | $P < 0.001$ | $P < 0.001$ |
| A. Mclean | | | | |
| (a) Prisoners | 569 | $6.65 \pm 3.12$ | $12.47 \pm 3.67$ | $11.77 \pm 4.98$ |
| (b) Controls | 595 | $4.38 \pm 2.32$ | $11.54 \pm 3.62$ | $8.82 \pm 4.50$ |
| | | $P < 0.001$ | $P < 0.001$ | $P < 0.001$ |

activity, the two groups overlap possibly to quite a large extent, and hence the differences between them will in truth be much larger than those that emerge from the statistical analysis. In spite of this weakness, this is obviously a valuable paradigm, and we will mention a number of other studies following this paradigm presently. Another difficulty with this paradigm is that personality variables may be affected by incarceration. Both problems are averted by making use of self-reported acts of delinquency and antisocial behavior (Hindelang, Hirschi, and Weis, 1979, 1981). An example of work using self-reports are studies by Allsopp and Feldman (1976).

Allsopp and Feldman used two different indices of antisocial behavior. The first of these is the self-report measure of antisocial behavior (ASB). This subjective index is supplemented by objective records of classroom detention and other punishments inflicted by teachers for misbehavior (Na, naughtiness score). For all the groups studied by Allsopp and Feldman, these two indices were found to correlate together quite well and to give similar personality differences between normal and antisocial children. This fact gives us confidence that the apparent subjectivity of the ASB questionnaire does not preclude considerable empirical validity.

In a first study Allsopp and Feldman (1974) studied four groups of subjects; 197 subjects took part, and the major outcome of the study is shown in figure 4. This groups together children who show high scores on none, one, two, or all three of the personality scales (P, E, and N); on the abscissa are given the mean ASB and Na scores for the four groups. It will be seen that there is a linear or at least monotonic increase in antisocial behavior with increase in P, E, and N; all three scales contribute about equally to the total result.

In a second study Allsopp and Feldman (1976) used 385 boys ranging in age from 11 to 16; they were tested in a grammar school. The analysis in this case was carried out for individual items of the various personality scales, which makes summary of the results somewhat difficult. However, as far as P is concerned, it was found that all seventeen P items differentiated between high and low ASB scores in the predicted manner. On E, all but three of the items differentiated the groups in the predicted manner, the only one showing more than minimal discrimination in the wrong direction being concerned with participation in hobbies and interests, a finding easily explained. On N, the hypothesis is upheld for most items, but there are several that do not conform, for reasons that are explained by the authors. However, it would be safe to assume from this and other studies that the importance of N is greater for older subjects and lesser for schoolchildren. The general outcome of this study cross-validates the results reported in the earlier work.

Allsopp and Feldman (1976) have reported one further study in which

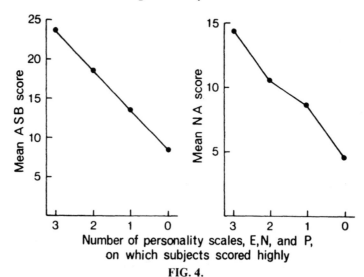

FIG. 4.

**Mean scores on Antisocial behaviour scale (ASB) and school misbehaviour (Naughtiness–NA) scales of children above average on one, two or all three of the P,E and N scales. After Eysenck, 1977.**

they used 461 children between the ages of 13 and 16; of these, results will be reported here on only the 368 white boys. Teachers were asked to rate the behavior of the boys; on this basis, they were divided into well-behaved and badly-behaved cohorts. When these ratings were compared with the personality scale scores, the results indicated that "badly-behaved boys predominate at the high level of P and at the low level of P where there is a combination of high E/high N scores; well-behaved boys predominate at the low level of P except where E and N are simultaneously high." When we turn to the ASB, we may use a factor analysis subdivision of the scale into ten factors. All the correlations with P, E, and N were positive, being highest with P and lowest with N. The results certainly bear out the general hypothesis in considerable detail.

A follow-up study to the Allsopp and Feldman study has been reported by Rushton and Chrision (1981), using eight separate samples of high school and university students, totaling 410. Self-report, paper-and-pencil questionnaire measures of both personality and delinquency were administered under conditions that ensured anonymity. The evidence showed clear support for the relationship between high delinquency scores and high scores on both extraversion and psychoticism. These relationships held up across diverse samples and different ways of analyzing the data. No support was found for a relationship between delinquency scores and the dimension of neuroticism.

Another replication has been reported by Silva, Martorell, and Clemente (1986) in Spain. An adaptation of the Allsopp and Feldman ASB, the junior version of the EPQ, and the Eysenck and Eysenck (1985) scale of impulsivity, venturesomeness, and empathy were administered to a population of children and adolescents. Results of analysis for three groups of low, medium, and high ASB scorers are given in Table 2. It can be seen that both on test and retest the high (antisocial) scorers are significantly higher on P, E, and N; lower on the lie scale (which in this case can probably be regarded as a measure of conformity); and higher on the criminality scale (Saklofske, McKerrqacher, and Eysenck, 1978), which combines the items in the EPQ most diagnostic of antisocial behavior. High ASB scores are also very significantly higher on impulsivity and venturesomeness, and lower in empathy.

Table 3 shows the results of the study in terms of correlations, for boys and girls separately, and for test and retest separately. Also given are the test-retest reliabilities of the various scales. The results show pretty clearly that P has the highest correlations with the ASB scale, particularly for the boys, with E and N having higher correlations for the girls. The L scale, measuring conformity in this group rather than dissimulation, has very high correlations (negative) particularly for girls, and the criminality scale also has high correlations for both. Impulsivity is clearly correlated with the ASB scale, venturesomeness less so, and empathy has a negative correlation, but negligibly small for girls, reasonably high for boys. In view of the rather low reliability of the trait measures, all these correlations would be much higher if corrected for attenuation. All in all, the figures leave little

**TABLE 2**
**ANOVA for 3 groups: Low ASB (N = 72), Medium ASB (N = 250),**
**and High ASB (N = 81). Deviations from means. From Silva et al. 1986.**

|  | Low | Medium ASB Test: | High |  | Low | Medium ASB Retest: | High |  |
|---|---|---|---|---|---|---|---|---|
|  |  |  |  | P < |  |  |  | P < |
| P | − 1.38 | − 0.26 | 1.90 | .01 | − 1.36 | − .46 | 2.38 | .001 |
| E | − .48 | − .19 | 0.89 | .05 | − 1.15 | .09 | .80 | .01 |
| N | − 1.14 | − .06 | 1.17 | .01 | − 1.90 | .25 | 1.10 | .001 |
| L | 2.95 | 44 | 4.58 | .001 | 2.60 | .61 | − 4.66 | .001 |
| C | − 1.99 | − .47 | 2.96 | .001 | 3.09 | − .31 | 3.54 | .001 |
| Imp. | − 2.52 | − .47 | 3.42 | .001 | − 3.31 | − .07 | 3.11 | .001 |
| Vent. | − 2.05 | .17 | 1.40 | .001 | − 1.71 | .20 | 1.02 | .001 |
| Em. | .71 | .33 | 1.45 | .001 | .55 | .50 | 1.70 | .001 |

ANOVA for 3 groups: Low ASB (N = 72), Medium ASB (N = 250), and Hgh ASB (N = 81). Deviations from mean.

TABLE 3
Reliability of scales test-retest used in Silva et al.,
1986 and corrections with ASB.

| Test-retest Reliability | | ASB Boys (N = 174) | | Girls (N = 183) | |
|---|---|---|---|---|---|
| | | Test | Retest | Test | Retest |
| P | .56 | .44 | .51 | .43 | .32 |
| E | .69 | .05 | .07 | .21 | .21 |
| N | .63 | .17 | .15 | .24 | .29 |
| L | .75 | −.47 | −.49 | −.62 | −.61 |
| C | .55 | .42 | .53 | .47 | .40 |
| Imp. | .68 | .43 | .42 | .47 | .54 |
| Vent. | .70 | .26 | .16 | .29 | .35 |
| Emp. | .69 | −.32 | −.35 | −.12 | −.02 |

doubt that there is a strong relationship between antisocial behavior, as reported by the children themselves, and personality. The test-retest reliability of the ASB scale is .67, so that correction for attenuation in the criterion might also be advisable.

How much difference would correction for attenuation make in these data? Let us consider a test correlating .50 with the ASB scale, with a test-retest reliability of .70. Corrected for attenuation, the correlation of the test with ASB scores would rise from .50 to .72, doubling the validity (.502 x 2 .722). This suggests that several of the personality scales share half the total variance with the ASB scale. It can hardly be said that this is not a valuable and important item of information.

Jamison (1980) obtained very similar results to those of Silva et al. (1986) in a study of 1,282 white children in secondary schools in England. Correlations between the ASB scale for boys and girls separately with a junior EPQ are reported in table 4; it again can be seen that the highest correlations are with P and L (negative); those with E are reasonably high, those with N quite small but still positive.

A particularly large and well-designed study has been reported by Powell (1977; Powell and Stewart, 1983). The subjects were 808 white nondelinquent children in ordinary schools, a total of 381 boys and 427 girls, subdivided into six groups from 8 at the bottom to 15 at the top. For some

TABLE 4
Correlations of ASB with personality variables, from Jamison, 1980.

| | N | P: | E: | N: | L: |
|---|---|---|---|---|---|
| Boys | 781 | .58 | .31 | .10 | −.56 |
| Girls | 501 | .59 | .40 | .09 | −.60 |

analyses a division was made between all senior and all junior children, with average ages of 13 and 9, respectively. Children were given the junior EPQ and a social-attitude test measuring religiosity, ethnocentrism, punitiveness, sex and hedonism, and conservatism. There were also administered a version of the ASB and a teacher's rating scale meant to measure general level of disturbance, antisocial behavior, and neurotic behavior. The main results of this study, insofar as they are relevant to this chapter, are seen in table 5. Correlations of the ASB scale, as in other studies, are highest with P and (negatively) with L. Correlations with E and N are in the expected direction, but lower. Powell subdivided extraversion into two factors, impulsivity and sociability, following the suggestion often made that impulsivity is more important for antisocial behavior than is sociability. "There was ... absolutely no evidence that the Impulsivity aspect of E is more related to criminality than is the Sociability factor. Neither Impulsivity nor Sociability correlate better with misbehaviour than does the E scale as a whole. It could be argued that treating E as two factors is only relevant when dealing with a prison population when unsociability measures are directly affected by their restricted environment" (p. 38).

Powell also followed up the suggestion by Burgess (1972) that a combina-

### TABLE 5
#### Correlations of P, E, N and L with ASB, from Powell, 1977.

Correlations of personality variables with anti-social behaviour

| | Age | PB | EB | Correlation NB | LB |
|---|---|---|---|---|---|
| Boys | 15 yr | 0.51** | 0.41** | 0.32* | −0.48** |
| | 13 yr | 0.52** | 0.52** | 0.34 | −0.61** |
| | 11 yr | 0.48** | 0.07 | 0.18 | −0.59** |
| | 10 yr | 0.42** | 0.19 | −0.04 | −0.52** |
| | 9 yr | 0.51** | −0.17 | 0.09 | −0.43** |
| | 8 yr | 0.32* | 0.17 | 0.34* | −0.42** |
| | Senior | 0.47** | 0.26** | 0.18* | −0.64** |
| | Junior | 0.42** | 0.04 | 0.09 | −0.48** |
| Girls | 15 yr | 0.57** | 0.12 | 0.39** | −0.59** |
| | 13 yr | 0.55** | 0.38** | 0.13 | −0.59** |
| | 11 yr | 0.13 | 0.04 | 0.33** | −0.31** |
| | 10 yr | 0.47** | −0.02 | 0.07 | −0.50** |
| | 9 yr | 0.58** | 0.26** | 0.17 | −0.47** |
| | 8 yr | 0.31 | −0.04 | 0.38* | −0.62** |
| | Senior | 0.44** | 0.17* | 0.30** | −0.56** |
| | Junior | 0.48** | 0.10 | 0.17* | −0.50** |

tion of high E and high N predicts antisocial behavior better than the scales taken separately, and that the formula h (hedonism) $-$ E $\times$ N might be used, where h would predict criminality. For senior and junior boys, the values for h were .30 and .12; for girls, .37 and .20. Clearly, the values are higher for senior boys and girls, and assume a reasonable size, although still lower than they are for P.

Using stepwise multiple regression techniques, Powell found multiple correlations for senior and junior boys, and senior and junior girls of .72, .54, .64, and .61, respectively. "The size of these correlations indicates the high degree with which personality predicts self-reported misbehaviour, it being difficult, in fact, to see how the correlations could be much higher unless the reliability of the scales could be substantially improved, with a concomitant reduction in errors of measurement" (p. 38).

Powell reports correlations between the ASB scale and social attitudes, which are of some interest. Table 6 shows these correlations; it will be seen that they are negative with conservatism and religiosity but positive with ethnocentrism, punitiveness, and sex and hedonism. The direction of the correlations is not perhaps surprising, but their size is probably greater than would have been expected.

## TABLE 6
### Correlations of social attitudes with ASB, from Powell, 1977

| Boys at age | Correlation | | | | |
|---|---|---|---|---|---|
| | B Con | B REL | E ETH | B PUN | B SEX |
| 15 yr | $-0.47**$ | $-0.40**$ | 0.24 | 0.25* | 0.41** |
| 13 yr | $-0.38**$ | $-0.28*$ | 0.20 | 0.27* | 0.47** |
| 11 yr | $-0.16$ | $-0.29*$ | 0.29* | 0.34** | 0.27* |
| 10 yr | $-0.43**$ | $-0.23*$ | 0.04 | 0.16 | 0.36** |
| 9 yr | $-0.25*$ | $-0.31**$ | 0.17 | 0.26* | 0.11 |
| 8 yr | $-0.29$ | $-0.06$ | $-0.13$ | 0.31* | 0.32* |
| Senior | $-0.40**$ | $-0.36**$ | 0.18* | 0.22** | 0.43** |
| Junior | $-0.36**$ | $-0.26**$ | 0.5 | 0.22** | 0.27** |
| Girls | | | | | |
| 15 yr | $-0.53**$ | $-0.47**$ | 0.36** | $-0.30*$ | 0.05 |
| 13 yr | $-0.63**$ | $-0.54**$ | 0.11 | 0.14 | 0.36** |
| 11 yr | $-0.20$ | $-0.15$ | 0.23* | 0.16 | 0.18 |
| 10 yr | $-0.33**$ | $-0.09$ | 0.04 | $-0.13$ | 0.19 |
| 9 yr | $-0.36**$ | $-0.25*$ | $-0.03$ | $-0.09$ | 0.22* |
| 8 yr | $-0.26$ | $-0.26$ | $-0.04$ | $-0.00$ | 0.06 |
| Senior | $-0.55**$ | $-0.47*8$ | $n-0.17*$ | $-0.00$ | 0.30** |
| Junior | $-0.32**$ | $-0.20**$ | $-0.01$ | $-0.08$ | 0.16* |

*P $<$ 0.05.
**P $<$ 0.01.

Among nonincarcerated adolescents the pattern is much the same as among children. R. Fogitt (1974) has recently published data on a non-institutionalized sample of delinquent and nondelinquent adolescents, 167 in all; these were administered a personality inventory including scales for the measurement of E and N, but not P. From analysis of the intercorrelations between the crimes and the personality scales, it became clear that they were all positively intercorrelated. A single general factor emerged from the analysis, on which different crimes had loadings as follows: truancy, 0.56; poor work history, 0.62; vagrancy, 0.71; attempted suicide, 0.56; frequency of violence, 0.74; destructiveness of violence, 0.72; heavy drinking, 0.45; excessive drugs, 0.52; theft, 0.71; fraud, 0.50; group delinquency, 0.46; number of convictions, 0.59; and E (0.44) and N (0.42). Age and social class were quite insignificantly related to the other variables (0.17 and 0.06). Clearly, for this group of adolescents also, E and N play an important part in relating to criminal activity. P was not included in the inventories used.

Further support for the hypothesis of personality factors being important in criminality comes from the extensive work of W. Belson (1975). In his large-scale inquiry into the criminal and antisocial behavior of 1,425 London boys, he sought evidence for the importance of certain factors often thought to be causal in the production of such behavior. He found strong evidence in favor of certain hypotheses relating to the personality of the boys involved in crime, such as "a desire for a lot of fun and excitement and a tendency to go out 'just looking for fun and excitement.'" This seems identical with our postulation of low arousal leading to a search for arousal-producing situations. "Permissiveness on the part of the boy in relation to stealing" was another, though less strong, factor; this would seem to correspond with our notion of a missing "conscience." "Frequent boredom" was another, though less strong, factor, as was a situation in which the boy's mother had always gone out to work. The former would be related to low arousal: the latter to low levels of conditioning (due to the absence of the person most concerned with carrying out the conditioning program). It was found that boys who engage in stealing are lacking in remorse over acts of theft; again supporting the "lack-of-conscience" hypothesis (Eysenck, 1977).

Association with boys who are already engaged in stealing was found to be an important cause; reasons for this association were that the boys concerned were friendly, lively, easy to get along with, fun—in other words, they were extraverted. It is interesting to note that the existence of a broken home (so frequently suggested as a causal factor) did not emerge as important, though a miserable or uninteresting home did. It seems likely that the latter acted through the intermediary of boredom and low arousal; the former, psychiatric views notwithstanding, failed to exert the supposed adverse influence.

Berman and Paisey (1984) investigated the relationship between anti-social behavior and personality in thirty juvenile males convicted of offenses of assault or confrontations with a victim, and thirty juvenile males convicted of offenses involving property without confrontation with the victim. Subjects were administered the EPQ and Zuckerman's Sensation-Seeking Scale. Juveniles convicted of assaultive offenses exhibited significantly higher P, E, and N scores, and lower lie scores than those convicted of property offenses only. Sensation-seeking scores were significantly lower for the nonassaultive group. These results show that even within a "criminal" group of juvenile offenders, severity of crime is still related in the prediction direction fashion to P, E, and N. How general are these findings? In other words, can we make cross-cultural comparisons that verify conclusions emerging essentially from Anglo-American countries?

Turning now to adult studies, with particular reference to cross-cultural comparisons, we must note first of all a meta-analysis reported by Steller and Hunze (1984) on fifteen empirical studies carried out in Germany, using the Freiburg Personality Inventory (FPI), which is a device measuring nine personality traits in addition to extraversion and neuroticism, and a masculinity scale. The E and N scales are comparable to those employed in the EPI, so that comparisons can be usefully made across countries. Altogether 3,450 delinquent subjects were used in these studies; full details about the works summarized by Steller and Hunze can be found in their article.

On primary trait scales delinquents have higher scores principally on depression, nervousness, excitability, and aggressiveness. In fifteen out of twenty-three comparisons delinquents have higher scores on emotional instability (neuroticism); similarly, extraversion is found more frequently in a delinquent than a nondelinquent group. Sociability was found significantly higher in extroverts in six out of twenty-three comparisons.

Steller and Hunze conclude that "delinquent compared with non-delinquent probands present themselves on the one hand as characterized by bad humor, low self regard, troubles with psychosomatic reactions, irritable and easily frustrated—altogether as emotionally liable—but on the other hand as spontaneously aggressive, emotionally under-developed, but also sociable and lively—altogether as extraverted" (p. 100).

With respect to age, there is some evidence of higher extraversion in juveniles, higher neuroticism in older delinquents, very much as found in the English-speaking samples.

Duration of incarceration did not seem to have any significant effect on the results of the questionnaire responses. This is an important item of information, contradicting the hypothesis often voiced that incarceration produces changes in personality.

The same conclusion is indicated by the fact that persons guilty of criminal conduct but not incarcerated show personality-scale deviations similar to those of the incarcerated. We see, thus, that a large number of investigations in Germany, mostly carried with adults, but some also with juvenile delinquents, using a different inventory from that used in the investigations so far discussed, give results very similar in nature. This is an important conclusion indicating evidence of cross-cultural validity for the theory in question.

Similar reasons have been found by Schwenkmetzger (1983) in a study of 107 delinquents, with German delinquents again appearing more neurotic, more aggressive, more depressive, more excitable, more impulsive, and more sensation seeking, and more ready to take risks. Differences on extraversion, though in the right direction, were not significant. Amelang and Rodel (1970) obtained similar results.

In addition to the studies carried out in Germany, Cote and Leblanc (1982) reported a study of 825 French adolescents between the ages of 14 and 19 who had filled in a personality inventory as well as a French version of the antisocial behavior scale. This scale was found to correlate very significantly with psychoticism (.36), and extraversion is more important than neuroticism. Equally clearly, results in France are similar to those in Great Britain, Germany, Spain, and other countries.

Continuing our survey of cross-culture studies, we turn next to India. The work carried out there is of particular interest because although it might be argued that Germany and France are sufficiently similar to Great Britain and other English-speaking countries to almost guarantee replication of results, India is sufficiently different to make it unlikely that results could be replicated if they were due largely to cultural factors. Narayanan and Mani (1977) tested fifty murderers, fifty ordinary criminals, and fifty normals and found that on various combinations of P, E, and N, along the lines suggested by Burgess (1972), murderers had the highest score; criminals, intermediate; and normals, the lowest.

Shammugam (1975) studied sixty-eight delinquent boys, seventy-three nondelinquent boys, sixty delinquent girls, and seventy-three nondelinquent girls. Using the EPI, differences found for P, E, and N are shown in Table 7. It will be clear that all are significant and in the expected direction.

Rahman and Husain (1984) studied seventy female prisoners in Bangladesh. The expected large differences were found for P and N; for E, there was no significant difference, but this is probably explained in terms of the large population of murderers with very low E scores. As Eysenck (1977) has pointed out, "Murderers (of the type that used to be predomi-

TABLE 7
P, E and N scores of delinquent and non-delinquent boys
and girls. Shanmugan, 1975.

| | P | | E | | N | |
|---|---|---|---|---|---|---|
| Delinquent boys | 8.60 | | 8.70 | | 13.20 | |
| | | (0.1) | | (0.1) | | (0.1) |
| Non-delinquent boys | 6.70 | | 6.61 | | 9.97 | |
| Delinquent girls | 8.40 | | 10.50 | | 13.20 | |
| | | (0.01) | | (.05) | | (.01) |
| Non-delinquent girls | 6.03 | | 9.30 | | 11.20 | |

Estimates of *P* in brackets.

nant until recently, i.e., done in the family, not terror murders and associated with armed robbery, now so common) tend to be introverted and repressed, until they suddenly break out of their shell" (p. 59). This view has of course been most prominently put forward by Edwin I. Megargee. It finds support in a study by Mani (1978), who compared thirty murderers in India with thirty-two nonmurderers. Murderers had very significantly lower extraversion scores, lower neuroticism scores, and lower psychoticism scores. The nonmurderers in this case were criminals committed for rape and robbery, not a normal, noncriminal sample. Compared to normal Indian samples, nonmurderer delinquents have higher scores on P, E, and N.

Singh (1980, 1982) reported on male and female juvenile delinquents who had been administered the EPI and the Catell NSQ. In both groups delinquents scored high on E and N. Similarly, Singh (1978, 1980) found that male and female truants scored higher on E and N than nontruants. Similar positive results are reported by Singh and Aktar (1971) and Aktar and Singh (1972) while Ramachandran (1970) found positive results for extraversion but not for neuroticism. All in all these studies tend to support the view that in India as well as in other countries criminality is linked with the same personality features.

All these studies and many others that have been discussed by Eysenck (1977) and Eysenck and Gudjonnson (in press) leave little doubt that there is quite a strong correlation between personality and criminality. Is this a causal relationship? The answer can be given only in terms of the possibility of prediction; in other words, is it possible to predict later criminality from earlier assessment of personality? The evidence suggests that the answer is in the affirmative.

The work of Burt (1965) is perhaps the most interesting. He reports on a follow-up of 763 children originally rated by their teachers for N and E more than thirty years previously. Fifteen percent and 18 percent, respectively, had become habitual criminals or neurotics. Of those who became habitual offenders, 63 percent had been rated as high on N; 54 percent, as high on E; only 3 percent, as high on introversion. Of those who became neurotics, 59 percent had been rated as high on N; 44 percent, as high on introversion; only 1 percent, as high on E. Thus, we see that even the probably rather unreliable ratings made by teachers of 10-year-old schoolboys can predict with surprising accuracy the later adult behavior of these children. Note also that these ratings took into account only two of the three major factors we have found associated with criminality; had ratings of P been included, it seems likely that the prediction would have been even more accurate.

Similar results have been reported by Michael (1956). Rather more doubtful, at first sight, seem the results reported by West and Farrington (1973). Their book reports a longitudinal survey of 411 boys who were aged 8-9 in 1961-62; they were given the Junior Maudsley Inventory in their primary school at age 10-11, and again in their secondary school at age 14-15. They were also given the EPI at age 16-17, when the majority of them had left school. Almost all the boys were tested at each age, and the book reports how the extraversion, neuroticism, and lie scores obtained at these three ages were related to juvenile delinquency, i.e. convictions in court for offenses committed between the boys' seventeenth and twenty-first birthdays (Farrington, 1976). Eighty-four boys were classified as juvenile delinquents, 94 as young adult delinquents, and 127 as delinquents at any age. Results are much more encouraging when related to these more extensive data.

As regards extraversion, there was a distinct tendency for boys with above-average E scores at age 16 to become young adult delinquents—30 percent as opposed to 16 percent, with P level at less than .005. The effect is largely due to the most introverted quarter's including significantly *fewer* adult delinquents. "This indicates that low E scores genuinely predict a low likelihood of adult delinquency."

As regards neuroticism, there was a significant tendency for those in the lower quarter of N scores at age 10 not to become adult delinquents, and not to be delinquents at any age. Furthermore, there was a significant tendency for those in the highest quarter of N scores at age 14 to be delinquents at any age.

As regards lie scores, those with below average L scores at age 10 were most likely to be delinquents at any age. "Dividing the L scores at this age into quarters showed the effect even more clearly. Of those in the highest quarter, only 19.8 percent were delinquents, in comparison with 44.1 percent of those in the lowest quarter." As Farrington points out, "These results back-up what we said in 'Who becomes Delinquent?,' namely that high L scores at age 10 probably did not reflect social desirability responses, but were obtained by well-behaved boys telling the truth." The L scores at ages 14 and 16 were not related to any of the delinquency classifications. A quadrant analysis was carried out, showing that "the stable introverts at age 10 included significantly fewer adult delinquents, and significantly fewer delinquents at any age, than the remainder. Neurotic extraverts at age 16 included significantly more adult delinquents, and significantly more delinquents at any age, than the remainder. The neurotic introverts at age 16 included significantly fewer adult delinquents than the remainder."

Farrington concludes his communication by saying that these data provided some support for the theory considered in this article: "In particular, if one takes the EPI scores at age 16, the extraverts were significantly more likely than the introverts to become adult delinquents, the neurotic extraverts were the most likely of all, and the neurotic introverts were at least likely of all. The results obtained with the NJMI at ages 10 and 14 are less clear-cut, but do include some supportive results."

These studies, taken in conjunction with those mentioned before that provided predictive data, do suggest that personality can be used as a predictor of future conduct with some degree of success, and considering the unreliabillity of all the elements entering into this equation, it seems clear that correction for attenuation would be appropriate in giving us a more realistic estimate of the true relationship obtaining, which would almost certainly be much closer than those published. For practical applications, of course, we must rest content with the uncorrected figures.

The other problem, already mentioned, is that of heterogeneity. There have been many attempts to sub-divide criminal populations into meaningful sub-groups. Gibbons (1975) gives a good review of these attempts, demonstrating that they, in turn, suffer from considerable heterogeneity; little agreement is in sight. Perhaps the application of factor analytic methods to this field may improve the situation; a study by Sinclair and Chapman (1973) suggests that this may indeed be so. We will return to their study after considering some recent attempts to investigate directly the homogeneity of prisoners' personality by means of cluster analysis.

McGurk and McDougall (1981) gave the EPQ to one hundred delinquent inmates of a detention center, and a group of normal youths roughly equal in age and background. The raw scores of the EPQ scales for both samples were each subjected to cluster analysis, resulting in the adoption of four-cluster solution for both the delinquent and the comparison groups. The clusters obtained from the delinquent group support the view that there are homogeneous subgroups in terms of personality profiles within a heterogeneous criminal sample, as there are in the comparison group. Consideration of the descriptions of the clusters in the two populations, however, shows that there are personality types appearing in the delinquent group that do not occur in the comparison group.

Both samples are similar in that they contain a high N, low E subgroup (D 1, C 1) and a low N, high E subgroup (D 2, C 2). The comparison group, however, also had a low N, low E subgroup (C 4) and a subgroup with high scores of P (C 3). This differs from the delinquent sample, which has a high N, high E subgroup (D 3) and a high P, high N and high E subgroup (E 4). Clearly subgroups D 3 and D 4, which occur only in the delinquent sample, are characterized by combinations of personality factors postulated by Eysenck's criminality theory. The other two groups are similar to those found among the controls, and would therefore not be covered by Eysenck's theory. McEwan (1983) used a similar method of analysis on a random group of 186 delinquents. Again a four-cluster solution was preferred. "The patterns of scores recorded by two of the clusters . . . are in line with direct predictions of Eysenck's theory of criminality. One cluster scores on P and E, while the other records high scores on E and N. Another subgroup records a high E score but this is accompanied by low scores on P and N. The remaining cluster has as its one defining characteristic a low E score and thus would appear to confound Eysenck's theory" (p. 202). It is interesting to note that the only subgroup characterized by a high P score proved to be the most heavily preconvicted.

In a later study McEwan and Knowles (1984) carried out another cluster analysis, and compared the resulting clusters for age and previous convictions, and across both types of offenses committed in the situational variables operating at the time of the more serious current offense in each category. Again, four clusters were indicated by these statistical analyses. Again, it was found that the high-P-scoring cluster had the highest number of previous convictions, and the low-P-scoring cluster the fewest. No differences were found across offenses or situational-context variables. Another multidimensional approach to the problem is presented by Wardell and Yeudall (1980) also using cluster analysis. They too ended up with four groups: primary and secondary psychopaths; subcultural psychopaths; overcontrolled; and violent aggressive groups, both high on inhibition.

These cluster-analysis studies suggest that although some clusters agree with predictions from Eysenck's theory, others do not, and occur equally among noncriminal groups. A possible solution to the problem is given by Sinclair and Chapman (1973), who carried out a factor analytic study of prisoners that resulted in two major factors. The components they found are relatively easy to interpret. The first seemed to them to represent the dimension of working-class criminality corresponding to that found by Marcus (1960) in his study of prisoners at Wakefield. A high scorer on this dimension would tend to be young, not particularly intelligent, and given to drink, violence, and committing offenses with his mates. He would tend to have truanted from school and to have low occupational status. This is a type of criminal who fits well into the Eysenck scheme.

The second component seems to describe a social inadequacy dimension. The social inadequate on this dimension would tend to be an older, neurotic, introverted individual, with a psychiatric history and poor contact with his wife and family. He would tend to commit his offenses on the spur of the moment, and sometimes violently while drunk. In general he would conform to West's (1963) description of the inadequate, although he could belong to either the active or passive variety.

Eysenck (1977) already drew attention to the existence of a large group of inadequates among prison populations, and pointed out that the theory, as far as extraversion was concerned, did not apply to them, and that they would be more likely to be introverted in character. The Sinclair and Chapman study does indeed show that although their first component has a positive loading on extraversion, the second component has a very significant negative loading of − .35. Thus, it is possible that in general the active type of criminal is more numerous in the samples studied but in a few studies the inadequate may be more numerous, giving rise to a negative correlation with extraversion in these groups. This is certainly a differentiation that should be borne in mind in all future studies. It seems to be the most important factor making for heterogeneity as far as the relationship between personality and criminality is concerned.

Our final study in relation to heterogeneity may be of interest. Eysenck, Rust, and Eysenck (1977) have studied five groups of criminals characterized by their respective crimes as common offenders, property offenders, violent offenders, inadequates, and a residual group guilty of different types of offenses. Figure 5 shows the resulting differentiation in terms of scores on the P, E, and N scales of the EPQ. The common offenders are offenders low on P, low on N, and high on E, whereas inadequates are high on P, high on N, and low on E.

The same study, using EPQ and GSR data for these five groups, showed in a discriminant function analysis a clear separation of the five groups of offenders (figure 6). These results suggest that in addition to a general factor of antisocial behavior, there are specific factors leading to different *types* of reaction. These also have correlates in personality, and will be discussed briefly later.

We are now in a position to summarize, at least tentatively, the large amount of data discussed in this chapter. The following conclusions seem to be justified. (1) There exists a general behavior pattern of antisocial behavior and criminality, marking the opposite end of a continuum to that constituted by prosocial altruistic behavior (Rushton, 1980). (2) Within the

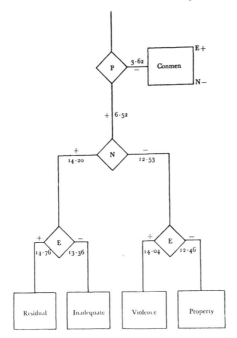

**FIG. 5.**
**P,E and N scores of criminals in 5 different crime
groups. Agter Eysenck, Rust & Eysenck, 1977.**

antisocial and criminal type of behavior there is a certain amount of heterogeneity, marked particularly by the opposition between active and inadequate criminals, but probably also including differences according to type
of crime committed. (3) Criminality is related to certain dimensions of

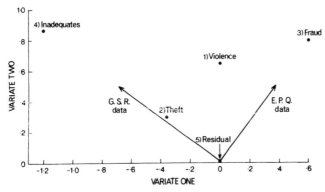

**FIG. 6.**
**Discriminant function analysis of five different crime
groups. After Eysenck, Rust & Eysenck, 1977.**

personality, in particular that labeled psychoticism, which is apparent in all age groups, and under all conditions studied. (4) There is a strong tendency for extraversion to be related to criminality, particularly in younger samples, and among more active criminals; inadequate older criminals do not show high extraversion, and may indeed be below average on this trait. (5) Most criminals are characterized by a high degree of neuroticism, but this may not be found as markedly in children and youngsters. (6) Scores on the L scale (regarded in these studies as a measure of conformity rather than of dissimulation) tend to correlate negatively with antisocial and criminal conduct, both in children, and in adolescents and adults. (7) The criminality scale, made up of the most diagnostic items of the EPQ, tends to discriminate significantly between criminals and noncriminals. (8) Primary personality traits, such as impulsiveness, venturesomeness, risk taking, empathy, and others, correlate in predictable directions with antisocial and criminal conduct. (9) These relationships are observed also in conditions where self-report of antisocial behavior is the major criterion; thus, personality-criminality relations are not confined to legal definitions of crime. (10) The observed personality-criminality correlations have cross-cultural validity, appearing in different countries and cultures with equal prominence. (11) Personality traits characteristic of antisocial and criminal behavior are also found correlated with behavior that is not criminal, but is regarded as antisocial, such as smoking. Drug users, whether legal (cigarette smoking) or illegal, tend to show high P, E, and N scores (Shammugam, 1975). Studies by Gossop (1978) and his associates show high P and N scores among drug users, but E scores are elevated only among drug users convicted of other crimes. The results summarized above are incompatible with a purely situational analysis of criminal behavior, and suggest an important contribution by dispositional factors.

## References

Aktar, S.N., and U.P. Singh. 1972. "The Temporary Stability of M.P.I. Scores in Normal and Criminal Populations." *Behaviour Metrica* 2:2-26.
Allsopp, J.F., and M.P. Feldman. 1974. "Extraversion, Neuroticism, Psychoticism and Antisocial Behaviour in School Girls." *Journal of Social Behaviour and Personality* 2: 184-90.
———. 1976. "Personality and Anti-social Behaviour in School Boys: Item Analysis of Questionnaire Measures." *British Journal of Criminology* 16: 337-51.
Amelang, M., and G. Rodel. 1970. "Personlichkeits undeinstellungskorrelate noinineller verhaltenweisen." *Psychologische Rundschau* 21: 157-79.
Belson, W. 1975. *Juvenile Theft: The Causal Factors.* New York: Harper & Row.
Berman, T., and T. Paisey. 1984. "Personality in Assaultive and Non-assaultive Juvenile Male Offenders." *Psychological Reports* 54: 527-30.

Burgess, P.K. 1972. "Eysenck's Theory of Criminality: A New Approach." *British Journal of Criminality* 12: 74-82.

Burt, C. 1965. "Factorial Studies of Personality and Their Bearing on the Works of the Teacher." *British Journal of Educational Psychology* 35: 308-18.

Cote, G., and M. Leblanc. 1982. "Aspects de personalite et comportement delinquent." *Bulletin de Psychologie* 36: 265-71.

Eysenck, H.J. 1977. *Crime and Personality.* 3d ed. London: Routledge & Kegan Paul.

Eysenck, H.J., and P. Barratt. 1985. "Psychophysiology and the Measurement of Intelligence." In *Methodological and Statistical Advances in the Study of Individual Differences,* edited by C.R. Reynolds and V.L. Wilson, New York: Plenum Press.

Eysenck, H.J., and G. Gudjonnson. In press. *The Causes and Cures of Crime.* New York: Plenum Press.

Eysenck, M.W., and H.J. Eysenck. 1985. *Personality and Individual Differences: A Natural Science Approach.* New York: Plenum Press.

Eysenck, S.B.G., J. Rust, and H.J. Eysenck. 1977. "Personality and the Classification of Adult Offenders." *British Journal of Criminology* 17: 169-79.

Farrington, D.P. 1976. Personal communication dated 10 June.

Gibbons, D.C. 1975. "Offender Typologies—Two Decades Later." *British Journal of Criminology* 15: 140-56.

Gossip, M. 1978. "Drug Dependence, Crime and Personality among Female Addicts. *Drug and Alcohol Dependence* 3: 359-64.

Hindelang, M.J., T. Hirschi, and J.G. Weiss. 1981. *Measuring Delinquency.* London: Sage Publications.

Jamison, R.N. 1980. "Psychoticism, Deviancy Perception of Risk in Normal Children." *Personality and Individual Differences* 1: 87-91.

McEwan, A.W. 1983. "Eysenck's Theory of Criminality and the Types of Offenses of Young Delinquents." *Personality and Individual Differences* 4: 201-4.

McEwan, A.W., and C. Knowles, 1984. "Delinquent Personality Type and Situational Contexts of Their Crimes." *Psychology and Individual Differences* 5: 339-44.

McGurk, B.J., and C. McDougall. 1981. "A New Approach to Eysenck's Theory of Criminality." *Personality and Individual Differences* 2: 388-40.

Mani, K. 1978. "A Comparative Study of Murderers and Violent Criminals Using Eysenck's Personality Inventory." *Indian Journal of Criminology* 6: 41-44.

Marcus, B. 1960. "A Dimensional Study of a Prison Population." *British Journal of Criminality* 1: 130-53.

Michael, C.M. 1956. "Follow-up Studies of Introverted Children, IV.: Relative Incidence of Criminal Behavior." *Journal of Criminal Law and Criminality* 47: 414-22.

Narayanan, S., and K. Mani, 1977. "A Measure of Set (Expectancy) in terms of Motion and Its Relation to Extroversion-Introversion and Psychoticism." *Journal of Psychological Researches* 19: 41-45.

Passingham, R.E. 1972. "Crime and Personality: A Review of Eysenck's Theory." In *Biological Basis of Individual Behaviour,* edited by V.D. Nebylitsyn and J.A. Gray. London: Academic Press.

Powell, G.E. 1977. "Psychoticism and Social Deviancy in Children." *Advances in Behaviour Research and Therapy* 1: 27-36.

Powell, G.E., and R.A. Stewart. 1983. "The Relationship of Personality to Antisocial and Neurotic Behaviours as Observed by Teachers." *Personality and Individual Differences* 4: 97-100.

Rahman, A., and A. Husain. 1984 "Personality and Female Criminals in Bangladesh." *Personality and Individual Differences* 5: 473-74.

Ramachandran, V. 1970. "An Experimental Study of the Behaviour Patterns of Criminals and Neurotics." Ph.D. dissertation, University of Kerala.

Rushton, J.P. 1980. *Altruism, Socialization and Society*. Englewood Cliffs, N.J.: Prentice-Hall.

Rushton, J.P., and R.D. Chrision. 1981. "Extraversion, Neuroticism, Psychoticism, and Self-reported Delinquency: Evidence from Eight Separate Samples." *Personality and Individual Differences* 2: 11-20.

Saklofske, D.H., D.W. McKerrqacher, and S.B.G. Eysenck. 1978. "Eysenck's Theory of Criminality: A Scale of Criminal Propensity as a Measure of Antisocial Behaviour." *Psychological Reports* 43: 683-86.

Schwenkmetzger, P. 1983. "Risikoverhalten, disikobereitschaft und delinquenz: Theoretische grundlagen und differential diagnostische untersuchungen." *Zeitschrift für Differentielle und Diagnostische Psychologie* 4: 223-29.

Shammugam, T.E. 1975. "A Study of Personality Patterns among Delinquents." *Indian Journal of Criminology* 3: 7-10.

Silva, F., C. Martorell, and A. Clemente. 1986. "Socialization and Personality: Study through Questionnaires in a Pre-adult Spanish Population." *Personality and Individual Differences* 7: 355-72.

Sinclair, I., and B. Chapman. 1973. "A Typologic and Dimensional Study of a Sample of Prisoners." *British Journal of Criminology* 13: 341-53.

Singh, A. 1978. "A Study of Personality of Truants." *Indian Journal of Clinical Psychology* 5: 179-84.

———. 1980a. "A Study of Personality and Adjustment of Female Juvenile Delinquents." *Child Psychiatry Quarterly* 13: 52-59.

———. 1980b. "Personality of Female Truants." *Child Psychiatry Quarterly* 3: 60-66.

Singh, U.P., and S.N. Aktar. 1971. "Criminals and Non-Criminals: A Comparative Study of Their Personality." *Indian Journal of Psychology* 46: 257-63.

Steller, M., and D. Hunze. 1984. "Zur selbstbeschreibung von delinquenten in freiburger personlichkeitsinventar (FBI)-line sekundaranalyse empirischer untersuchungen." *Zeitschrift für Differentielle und Diagnostische Psychologie* 5: 87-109.

Wardell, D., and L.T. Yeudall. 1980. "A Multi-dimensional Approach to Criminal Disorders: The Assessment of Impulsivity and Its Relation to Crime." *Advances in Behaviour Research and Therapy* 2: 159-77.

West, D., and D.P. Farrington. 1963. *Who Becomes Delinquent?* London: Heinemann.

# 7

# Japan: A Country with Safe Streets

## Gideon Fishman and Simon Dinitz

Two ideal typical models of criminal justice system assumptions, policies, and practices have been analyzed by Herbert Packer (1969) in his *The Limits of the Criminal Sanction*. These models are the Crime Control and the Due Process conceptions. In common, both models set as their primary goal the prevention of crime and deviance. So much for the commonality.

In describing these conceptions, Packer likens the Crime Control model to an assembly line and the Due Process model to an obstacle course. Law enforcement is the key element in the Crime Control model. The police apprehend factually guilty or probably guilty suspects, and other actors— prosecutors, judges, defense counsel—play their preassigned roles in converting *factual* into *legal* guilt as expeditiously as possible within the framework of the legal (adversarial) system. Anything that interferes with either the enforcement or the processing of arrestees through the prosecutorial, judicial, or correctional branches cannot be tolerated. In contrast, the Due Process model begins with the assumption that each phase in the funnel from probable factual guilt (arrest) to established legal guilt (conviction) must be strewn with obstacles. Only the surmounting of these obstacles makes it certain or almost certain that suspects whose cases result in conviction and penal sanction are truly deserving of this outcome. To adherents of the Due Process model, whatever else the system does nor does not do, it must never tolerate the conviction of innocents.

Hence, the Due Process model compels the strictest adherence to court-interpreted constitutional prescriptions and proscriptions—*Miranda* warnings, search and seizure rules, pretrial confinement and preventive detention restrictions, and the various other prohibitions, implicit or explicit, found in the various amendments dealing with speech and assembly, self-incrimination, the right to counsel, and cruel and unusual punishment. In the Due Process model there can never be quite enough legal impediments to balance the might of the state. Although the protection of society must be a primary goal, the ultimate goal must be the protection of the individual rights of suspects, of those already convicted and of those being sanctioned.

Thus, Packer observes that the Control model operates like an assembly line, putting output (quantity) above occasional error, and that the Due Process model puts the elimination of occasional or probable error (quality control, he calls it) above the efficient processing of cases. Writes Packer (1969), in a most lucid depiction of the difference in emphasis that can also serve as a summary of the Due Process model:

> By forcing the state to prove its case against the accused in an adjudication context, the presumption of innocence serves to force into play all the qualifying and disabling doctrines that limit the use of the criminal sanction against the individual. . . . By opening up a procedural situation that permits the successful assertion of defenses having *nothing* to do with factual guilt, it vindicates the proposition that the factually guilty may nonetheless be legally innocent; and should therefore be given a choice to qualify for that kind of treatment [167].

Elsewhere in his analysis Packer states the essence of the Control model:

> In theory, the Crime Control model can tolerate rules that forbid illegal arrests, unreasonable searches, coercive interrogations and the like. What it cannot tolerate is the vindication of those rules in the criminal process itself through the exclusion of evidence illegally obtained or through the reversal of convictions in cases where the criminal process has breached the rules laid down for its observance [Packer, 1969:168].

As its detractors rightly assert, the Due Process model is oppositional— just like the obstacle course to which it is likened. Its more extreme detractors also assert that this model *is more centrally concerned with compelling social control agents to toe the mark than in compelling offenders to do the same.* In contrast, the Social Control model is said to be affirmative in its approach to the apprehension, processing, and conviction of the factually guilty in so expeditious and unimpeded manner as to be considered unthinkable in the Due Process model.

To a greater or lesser extent, the U.S. commitment to the Due Process model has flourished even in areas of judicial conservatism and of public and political pressures to increase the efficiency of the law enforcement sector (by removing due process impediments) and the credibility of the penal sanction (Van den Haag, 1975). From the end of World War II to about 1975 the criminal justice apparatus was greatly circumscribed in its functions by an activist Supreme Court dedicated to insuring increasing equality before the law by race, class, and sex and by redressing the criminal justice equation in favor of the lowly individual in relation to the powerful state.

The U.S. affinity, in all sorts of political climates, for the due process model hardly needs extensive exposition. Nourished in the principles of the French Revolution, which, on the American soil, neatly complemented the Protestant ethic laissez-faire motif, a nation of outcasts and strangers feared statism more than unbridled freedom, the fraternity of law enforcers as much and at times more than the fraternity of violators (de Tocqueville, 1945). Although the "crime-in-the-streets" issue may yet redress the balance in the preference for the Social Control over the Due Process model, the collective memory embedded in U.S. history is still the greater fear of the potential excess of enforcement than the real threat of crime. Any reasonable reading of constitutional history or legislative debates of the 1984 federal criminal code seems to validate the primacy of the fear of the social control apparatus over that of predatory crime. In view of this commitment to the protection to be afforded to each person under law, it is noteworthy that the Due Process model rights only recently were extended to blacks, Native Americans, and Hispanics, and to prisoners and other wards of the state. Adherence to this model clearly did not prevent the U.S. from interning the Japanese American community in World War II nor the systematic violations, under color of posing a real and present danger, of traditional due process assumptions and practices.

The U.S. commitment to due process is paralleled by Japan's equally hoary commitment to a *consensual* Social Control model of criminal justice. If anything, the Japanese are more consistent and far less troubled and dissatisfied with the functioning of their system than we are with ours. And, as we will show, the Japanese success in *reducing* its "safety-crime" rate but not organized crime, white-collar crime, and corruption in the past two decades is clear and convincing testimony that a culturally "suitable" model, a criminal justice system that delivers on its promises, can be successful in a dynamic industrial society. Japan is the single best advertisement for the effectiveness of the *consensual* as opposed to the *coercive* Social Control model featured in nearly all totalitarian states, whether of the Left or Right (Clifford, 1976).

Japan's success in containing its street-crime problem, despite postwar chaos and unusually rapid industrialization and modernization, can be documented in the White Paper on Crime issued by the Japanese government in 1977 and buttressed by reports to the UN Crime Prevention and Criminal Justice Branch, and at various international meetings of experts (Ministry of Justice, Japan, 1977).

Table 1 indicates that while the Japanese population of criminally responsible adults grew from 53 to 88 million in the years 1948 to 1977 inclusive, conventional offenses known to the police and local authorities *fell* from 2,995 to 1,437 per 200,000 criminally responsible adults. The number of suspects per 100,000 *fell* from 1,003 to 409; the number of persons prosecuted, from 444 to 161; and the number of persons convicted, from 427 to 118. Table 1 also shows that most of this decline occurred prior to 1970. Since then the rates of offenses known, and of offenders handled in the system, have declined less sharply. Still, this general decline occurred precisely when other developed countries were experiencing unprecedented increases in nearly every category of crime and especially in the safety offenses (Shinnar and Shinnar, 1975). The decrease in the rate of crime in Japan is not an artifact of changes in the Japanese penal code, of reporting and recording procedures, or of alterations in the processing of complaints. Insofar as any criminal justice data, from any country, can be used with confidence, these Japanese figures are undoubtedly more reliable than crime trend data from elsewhere. Few can disagree with the assertion that it is usually in the interest of every criminal justice system to increase the magnitude of the problem it confronts, if only for budgetary and personnel reasons, to say nothing of political pressures and motives. Thus, given this bias toward exaggeration of the crime problem, the Japanese trend line is even more impressive.

The overall Japanese crime rate was disaggregated into the major components of property, violent, heinous, sex, negligence, and miscellaneous offenses. It is noteworthy that only the property crime category showed a substantial increase 1973-77; the rate in all other categories fell dramatically. Using 1973 as the index year (100) the property crime rate rose to 108, 113, 115, and 118 through 1977—18 percent in the fifth year. Most of these yearly increases were caused by the greater numbers of theft (larceny) offenses reported and by a very substantial rise in the rate of reported embezzlements. In contrast, the number of violent offenses investigated by the police declined systematically and substantially from the index figure of 100 in 1973 to 93, 86, 80, and 79 in subsequent years. Comparing 1973 and 1977, the rate of reported violent crimes decreased no less than 21 percent, a figure bordering on phenomenal. "Heinous" crimes, within the crimes of violence category, also fell but not as sharply. The figures, following the index year of 1973 were 95, 106, 99, and 91. The sharpest decline of all, however, was in the sex offense rate. From 100 in 1973, the dropoff was 95, 91, 83, and 74 in succeeding years. All of these data, by specific category, are presented in Table 2.

Time comparisons are one thing, cross-national quite another. The Japanese White Paper (1977) contrasts its own natural reported crime rates for

TABLE 1
Non-Traffic Penal Code Offenders—Suspected, Prosecuted, and
Convicted: selected years (Computed per 100,000 Criminally
Responsible Population)

| Year | Criminally Responsible Population Unit: 1,000 | Rate Computed per 100,000 of the Criminally Responsible Population | | | |
|------|------|------|------|------|------|
| | | Offences Known | Suspects | Persons Prosecuted | Persons Convicted in the Court of First Instance |
| 1948 | 53,413 | 2,995 | 1,003 | 444 | 427 |
| 1955 | 61,443 | 2,337 | 799 | 297 | 254 |
| 1966 | 76,459 | 1,690 | 564 | 245 | 206 |
| 1969 | 79,740 | 1,570 | 470 | 204 | 167 |
| 1967 | 80,500 | 1,587 | 470 | 198 | 159 |
| 1971 | 81,364 | 1,526 | 442 | 182 | 148 |
| 1972 | 82,947 | 1,473 | 417 | 185 | 151 |
| 1973 | 83,885 | 1,416 | 423 | 166 | 137 |
| 1974 | 84,792 | 1,425 | 425 | 153 | 126 |
| 1975 | 86,323 | 1,428 | 419 | 170 | 118 |
| 1976 | 87,195 | 1,429 | 409 | 169 | 118 |
| 1977 | 88,145 | 1,437 | 409 | 161 | — |

Source: White Paper on Crime, Government of Japan, 1977

seven offenses with those of a group of developed countries (including Japan) and consisting of the United States, England, and West Germany, among other high economic growth countries. The developing countries category includes nations from Asia, Latin America, and Africa. The data were initially collected by the UN Crime Prevention and Criminal Justice Branch and cover the period 1970-75.

Most notable of all is the cross-national robbery comparison. In the developing countries the reported group rate was 58.8 per 100,000 population; in the developed countries, 33.3; in Japan, 2.1. The Japanese rate is also unique in the assault and the sex offense categories. And, the reported Japanese rate is half as high as the rate in the developing countries for homicide.

In direct comparison with the United States, Japan has less than a quarter of the U.S. murder rate, a fifth of the rape, and less than *1* percent (.95 percent) of the robbery rate. Reversed, the United States records 4.5 times as many murders, 5.0 times the rapes, and 105 times the number of robberies per 100,000 population (Dinitz, 1981).

## The Formal Social Control Process in Japan

To achieve these stunningly low rates of conventional crime in a society once sorely traumatized by the intrusion of Western ways (in the nine-

**TABLE 2**
**Trends in Penal Code Offenders Investigated by the Police by Crime Categories**
**1973-1980**

| OFFENSES | 1973 | 1974 |
|---|---|---|
| I. Property Offenses | | |
| 1. Theft | 174,003 | 190,792 |
| 2. Fraud | 15,908 | 15,118 |
| 3. Embezzlement | 8,809 | 7,735 |
| 4. Stolen property | 2,070 | 2,046 |
| 5. Breach of trust | 203 | 174 |
| Total | 200,273 | 215,865 |
| | | |
| II. Offenses of Violence | | |
| A. "Nonheinous" Crimes | | |
| 6. Assault | 32,408 | 31,415 |
| 7. Bodily injury (including those resulting in death) | 53,008 | 46,850 |
| 8. Intimidation | 2,199 | 1,977 |
| 9. Extortion | 11,930 | 11,602 |
| 10. Unlawful assembly with weapon | 1,006 | 1,660 |
| Total | 100,551 | 93,512 |
| B. "Heinous" Crimes | | |
| 11. Murder (including patricide, infanticide and attempt) | 2,113 | 1,870 |
| 12. Robbery | 910 | 840 |
| 13. Robbery involving homicide, bodily injury, or rape | 1,168 | 1,271 |
| Total | 4,191 | 3,981 |
| | | |
| III. Sex Offenses | | |
| 14. Rape (including those resulting injury and death) | 4,786 | 4,485 |
| 15. Indecent assault | 1,816 | 1,629 |
| 16. Obscene matters (distributing, selling, etc.) | 3,644 | 3,604 |
| Total | 10,246 | 9,718 |
| | | |
| IV. Offenses of Negligence | | |
| 17. Professional negligence causing death or bodily injury | 576,855 | 491,982 |
| 18. Simple Negligence causing death or injury | 546 | 519 |
| 19. Fire caused by negligence | 4,828 | 4,314 |
| Total | 582,229 | 496,815 |
| | | |
| V. Miscellaneous | | |
| 20. Arson | 702 | 748 |
| 21. Gambling | 15,631 | 16,020 |
| 22. Kidnapping | 224 | 178 |
| 23. Forgery and counterforgery | 1,857 | 1,645 |
| Total | 18,414 | 18,591 |

TABLE 2 (Continued)
Trends in Penal Code Offenders Investigated by the Police by Crime Categories
1973-1980

| OFFENSES | 1975 | 1976 |
|---|---|---|
| I. Property Offenses | | |
| 1. Theft | 198,423 | 201,932 |
| 2. Fraud | 16,603 | 15,918 |
| 3. Embezzlement | 8,647 | 9,904 |
| 4. Stolen property | 1,838 | 1,811 |
| 5. Breach of trust | 195 | 236 |
| Total | 225,706 | 229,801 |
| | | |
| II. Offenses of Violence | | |
| A. "Nonheinous" Crimes | | |
| 6. Assault | 27,822 | 26,368 |
| 7. Bodily injury (including those resulting in death) | 42,775 | 40,590 |
| 8. Intimidation | 1,989 | 1,700 |
| 9. Extortion | 12,367 | 10,686 |
| 10. Unlawful assembly with weapon | 1,206 | 1,038 |
| Total | 86,159 | 80,382 |
| B. "Heinous" Crimes | | |
| 11. Murder (including patricide, infanticide and attempt) | 2,179 | 2,113 |
| 12. Robbery | 936 | 939 |
| 13. Robbery involving homicide, bodily injury, or rape | 1,310 | 1,106 |
| Total | 4,425 | 4,158 |
| | | |
| III. Sex Offenses | | |
| 14. Rape (including those resulting in injury and death) | 4,052 | 3,394 |
| 15. Indecent assault | 1,570 | 1,465 |
| 16. Obscene matters (distributing, selling, etc.) | 3,654 | 3,653 |
| Total | 9,276 | 8,512 |
| | | |
| IV. Offenses of Negligence | | |
| 17. Professional negligence causing death or bodily injury | 468,502 | 473,638 |
| 18. Simple negligence causing death or injury | 470 | 410 |
| 19. Fire caused by negligence | 3,863 | 3,962 |
| Total | 472,835 | 478,010 |
| | | |
| V. Miscellaneous | | |
| 20. Arson | 736 | 876 |
| 21. Gambling | 14,673 | 12,539 |
| 22. Kidnapping | 176 | 144 |
| 23. Forgery and counterforgery | 1,888 | 2,147 |
| Total | 17,473 | 15,706 |

**TABLE 2 (Continued)**
**Trends in Penal Code Offenders Investigated by the Police by Crime Categories**
**1973-1980**

| OFFENSES | 1977 | 1978 |
|---|---|---|
| I. Property Offenses | | |
| 1. Theft | 207,064 | 231,403 |
| 2. Fraud | 15,665 | 16,594 |
| 3. Embezzlement | 12,375 | 14,157 |
| 4. Stolen property | 1,639 | 1,717 |
| 5. Breach of trust | 226 | 208 |
| Total | 236,969 | 264,079 |
| II. Offenses of Violence | | |
| A. "Nonheinous" Crimes | | |
| 6. Assault | 25,781 | 23,996 |
| 7. Bodily injury (including those resulting in death) | 40,730 | 36,423 |
| 8. Intimidation | 1,702 | 1,582 |
| 9. Extortion | 9,660 | 9,399 |
| 10. Unlawful assembly with weapon | 1,236 | 1,264 |
| Total | 79,109 | 72,664 |
| B. "Heinous" Crimes | | |
| 11. Murder (including patricide, infanticide and attempt) | 1,988 | 1,843 |
| 12. Robbery | 814 | 822 |
| 13. Robbery involving homicide, bodily injury, or rape | 1,013 | 926 |
| Total | 3,814 | 3,591 |
| III. Sex Offenses | | |
| 14. Rape (including those resulting in injury and death) | 3,046 | 2,876 |
| 15. Indecent assault | 1,540 | 1,482 |
| 16. Obscene matters (distributing, selling, etc.) | 2,947 | 3,094 |
| Total | 7,533 | 7,452 |
| IV. Offenses of Negligence | | |
| 17. Professional negligence causing death or bodily injury | 461,353 | 463,973 |
| 18. Simple negligence causing death or injury | 363 | 332 |
| 19. Fire caused by negligence | 3,791 | 3,586 |
| Total | 465,507 | 467,891 |
| V. Miscellaneous | | |
| 20. Arson | 921 | 944 |
| 21. Gambling | 12,238 | 10,595 |
| 22. Kidnapping | 136 | 140 |
| 23. Forgery and counterforgery | 1,805 | 2,065 |
| Total | 15,100 | 13,704 |

TABLE 2 (Continued)
Trends in Penal Code Offenders Investigated by the Police by Crime Categories
1973-1980

| OFFENSES | 1979 | 1980 |
|---|---|---|
| I. Property Offenses | | |
| 1. Theft | 233,872 | 248,389 |
| 2. Fraud | 12,795 | 13,492 |
| 3. Embezzlement | 15,714 | 20,595 |
| 4. Stolen property | 1,638 | 1,667 |
| 5. Breach of trust | 147 | 180 |
| Total | 264,166 | 284,323 |
| II. Offenses of Violence | | |
| A. "Nonheinous" crimes | | |
| 6. Assault | 20,272 | 21,362 |
| 7. Bodily injury (including those resulting in death) | 33,571 | 34,941 |
| 8. Intimidation | 1,383 | 1,352 |
| 9. Extortion | 8,202 | 8,640 |
| 10. Unlawful assembly with weapon | 1,382 | 1,859 |
| Total | 64,810 | 68,154 |
| B. ""Heinous" Crimes | | |
| 11. Murder (including patricide, infanticide and attempt) | 1,841 | 1,560 |
| 12. Robery | 813 | 985 |
| 13. Robbery involving homicide, bodily injury, or rape | 996 | 1,079 |
| Total | 3,650 | 3,624 |
| III. Sex Offenses | | |
| 14. Rape (including those resulting in injury and death) | 2,757 | 2,667 |
| 15. Indecent assault | 1,469 | 1,420 |
| 16. Obscene matters (distributing, selling, etc.) | 2,378 | 2,160 |
| Total | 6,604 | 6,247 |
| IV. Offenses of Negligence | | |
| 17. Professional negligence causing death or bodily injury | 474,126 | 479,572 |
| 18. Simple negligence causing death or injury | 191 | 185 |
| 19. Fire caused by negligence | 2,547 | 2,433 |
| Total | 476,864 | 482,190 |
| V. Miscellaneous | | |
| 20. Arson | 943 | 948 |
| 21. Gambling | 8,626 | 9,443 |
| 22. Kidnapping | 97 | 87 |
| 23. Forgery and counterforgery | 2,132 | 1,809 |
| Total | 11,798 | 12,287 |

TABLE 2 (Continued)
Trends in Penal Code Offenders Investigated by the Police
by Crime Categories 1973-1980

| OFFENSES | 1973 | 1974 | 1975 | 1976 |
|---|---|---|---|---|
| I. Property Offenses | | | | |
| 1. Theft | 100 | 110 | 114 | 116 |
| 2. Fraud | 100 | 95 | 104 | 100 |
| 3. Embezzlement | 199 | 96 | 107 | 122 |
| 4. Stolen property | 100 | 99 | 89 | 87 |
| 5. Breach of trust | 100 | 86 | 96 | 116 |
| Total | 100 | 108 | 113 | 115 |
| II. Offenses of Violence | | | | |
| A. "Nonheinous" Crimes | | | | |
| 6. Assault | 100 | 97 | 86 | 81 |
| 7. Bodily injury those resulting in death) | 100 | 88 | 81 | 77 |
| 8. Intimidation | 100 | 90 | 90 | 77 |
| 9. Extortion | 100 | 97 | 104 | 90 |
| 10. Unlawful assembly with death | 100 | 165 | 120 | 103 |
| Total | 100 | 93 | 86 | 80 |
| B. "Heinous" Crimes | | | | |
| 11. Murder (including patricide, infanticide and attempt) | 100 | 88 | 103 | 108 |
| 12. Robbery | 100 | 93 | 103 | 103 |
| 13. Robbery involving homicide, bodily injury, or rape | 100 | 109 | 112 | 95 |
| Total | 100 | 95 | 106 | 99 |
| III. Sex Offenses | | | | |
| 14. Rape (including those resulting in injury and death) | 100 | 94 | 85 | 71 |
| 15. Indecent assault | 100 | 90 | 86 | 81 |
| 16. Obscene matters (distributing, selling, etc.) | 100 | 99 | 100 | 100 |
| Total | 100 | 95 | 91 | 83 |
| IV. Offenses of Negligence | | | | |
| 17. Professional negligence causing death or bodily injury | 100 | 85 | 81 | 82 |
| 18. Simple negligence causing death o injury | 100 | 95 | 86 | 75 |
| 19. Fire caused by negligence | 100 | 89 | 80 | 82 |
| Total | 100 | 85 | 81 | 82 |
| V. Miscellaneous | | | | |
| 20. Arson | 100 | 107 | 105 | 125 |
| 21. Gambling | 100 | 102 | 94 | 80 |
| 22. Kidnapping | 100 | 79 | 79 | 64 |
| 23. Forgery and counterforgery | 100 | 89 | 102 | 116 |
| Total | 100 | 101 | 95 | 85 |

TABLE 2 (Continued)
Trends in Penal Code Offenders Investigated by the Police
by Crime Categories 1973-1980

| OFFENSES | 1977 | 1978 | 1979 | 1980 |
|---|---|---|---|---|
| I. Property Offenses | | | | |
| 1. Theft | 119 | 133 | 134 | 143 |
| 2. Fraud | 98 | 104 | 80 | 85 |
| 3. Embezzlement | 153 | 175 | 194 | 255 |
| 4. Stolen property | 79 | 83 | 79 | 82 |
| 5. Breach of trust | 111 | 102 | 72 | 89 |
| Total | 118 | 132 | 132 | 142 |
| II. Offenses of Violence | | | | |
| A. "Nonheinous" Crimes | | | | |
| 6. Assault | 80 | 74 | 63 | 66 |
| 7. Bodily injury (including those resulting in death) | 77 | 69 | 63 | 66 |
| 8. Intimidation | 77 | 72 | 63 | 61 |
| 9. Extortion | 81 | 79 | 69 | 72 |
| 10. Unlawful assembly with weapon | 123 | 126 | 137 | 185 |
| Total | 79 | 72 | 64 | 68 |
| B. "Heinous Crimes | | | | |
| 11. Murder (including patricide, infanticide and attempt) | 94 | 87 | 87 | 74 |
| 12. Robbery | 89 | 90 | 89 | 108 |
| 13. Robbery involving homicide, bodily injury, or rape | 87 | 79 | 85 | 92 |
| Total | 91 | 86 | 87 | 86 |
| III. Sex Offenses | | | | |
| 14. Rape (including those resulting in injury and death) | 64 | 60 | 58 | 56 |
| 15. Indecent assault | 85 | 82 | 79 | 78 |
| 16. Obscene matters (distributing, selling, etc.) | 81 | 85 | 65 | 59 |
| Total | 74 | 73 | 64 | 61 |
| IV. Offenses of Negligence | | | | |
| 17. Professional negligence causing death or bodily injury | 10 | 80 | 82 | 83 |
| 18. Simple negligence causing death or injury | 66 | 61 | 35 | 34 |
| 19. Fire caused by negligence | 79 | 74 | 53 | 50 |
| Total | 80 | 80 | 82 | 83 |
| V. Miscellaneous | | | | |
| 20. Arson | 131 | 134 | 134 | 135 |
| 21. Gambling | 78 | 68 | 55 | 60 |
| 22. Kidnapping | 61 | 63 | 43 | 39 |
| 23. Forgery and counterforgery | 97 | 111 | 115 | 97 |
| Total | 82 | 74 | 64 | 67 |

Justice Branch Report, 1977). The comparisons are shown in table 3.

TABLE 3
Rate of Major Crimes Known to the Police per 100,000 Population in Developed
and Developing Countries and in Japan, 1970-1975.

| Crime | Developing Countries Group | Developed Countries Group | Japan |
|---|---|---|---|
| Homicide | 5.1 | 2.7 | 2.1 |
| Assault | 253.1 | 115.3 | 49.9 |
| Sex offense | 24.3 | 24.0 | 5.8 |
| Kidnapping | 1.2 | 0.2 | 0.2 |
| Robbery | 58.8 | 33.3 | 2.1 |
| Theft | 354.3 | 1,370.5 | 927.3 |
| Fraud | 30.1 | 136.4 | 45.7 |

The figures are based on the UN First World Crime Survey.

teenth century), the humiliation, demoralization and destruction of World War II, and the subsequent "benign" U.S. occupation that ended only in 1952, Japan has relied on traditional and *consensual* methods of social control. In few spheres of Japanese life is the Social Control model more consciously or efficiently applied than in criminal justice; in fewer still with such conspicuous success. The Japanese do not permit any untidiness in their criminal justice system and the Due Process model with its personal guarantees and legal hurdles is nothing if not untidy. Japanese policy focuses on efficiency, professionalism, and a degree of publicly sanctioned invasion into personal affairs that is very nearly incomprehensible in Western societies. This intrusiveness has public support and cooperation, probably the key variable of all.

Unencumbered by concern with U.S. due process constraints on "lawful" search and seizure, arrest, interrogation, and other "taken-for-granted" entry-level rights of the suspect, the Japanese police "cleared-by-arrest" rate (a measure of police efficiency, and victim and spectator support) is remarkably high by U.S. standards (Bayley, 1976).

The "cleared-by-arrest" rate in the United States is roughly 22 percent and varies widely with offense type (Uniform Crime Reports, 1980). In Japan the comparable overall rate in the same year was 69 percent. The Japanese police "cleared" 77 percent of the reported robberies, 83 percent of the rapes, 96 percent of the murders, and 86 percent of the arson cases. The U.S. figures (1979) were murder, 73 percent; rape, 48 percent; robbery, 25 percent; burglary, 15 percent; and motor vehicle theft, 14 percent. There is simply no way to account for Japan's high clearance rates without highlighting the cooperativeness of the Japanese public. Beginning with clearance by arrest, the Japanese are relentless in their pursuit of a case through the criminal justice process to conviction. Once the latter is accomplished, the punishment is quite light, both for juveniles and adults. The Japanese system employs two of the three principles of the classicists: certainty (detection and arrest), celerity (speedy prosecution), and severity (punishment) (Beccaria, 1804; Bentham, 1830). Japanese sanctions are relatively modest. Experience, no less than theory, suggests that the severity of criminal sanction is often inversely related to arrest probability.

The Japanese have developed a police system featuring personal knowledge of the neighborhood and its people, and little gadgetry. There are about 6,000 ministations, each serving a catchment population of about 10,000 people in the cities. In the countryside there are some 10,000 ministations with a catchment population of 5,000 people each. These are called *chuzaisho* (Vogel, 1979). In addition, the police make rounds on foot and on bicycle. They are an integral part of the neighborhood scene. Consequently, law enforcement is local, immediate, and directly responsive to its constituency (Bayley, 1976). That was once the U.S. pattern and is still the preferred style of policing in England and in some other modern industrial nations.

The police are totally professional (Bayley, 1976). The profession is a "calling" and not just a job. Police recruits are enrolled in a *one*-year training program before assuming their duties. Those who "burnout" are moved out of direct street contact duties; those unfit or brutal or excessively zealous are summarily removed, i.e. fired. Citizen complaints are heard, investigated, and adjudicated. The "brotherhood" syndrome that characterizes U.S. policing agencies is insufficient in Japanese policing agencies to protect incompetents and men of poor judgment. Such a policy inspires public confidence rather than the overt hostility encountered in core neighborhoods in our largest cities.

Each resident in every household must be registered at the ministation. The police, therefore, know who belongs where. In theory, the local police visit every household twice a year to check the currency of residence-status information and changes in the household roster. This is considered no invasion of privacy but a very legitimate activity. The census taker-enforcement officer-service provider can hardly be viewed as an ogre in the context, especially to juveniles. In the process of census taking, the police update their information on car ownership, the possession of valuables, and other such items of information so as to facilitate the protection and recovery of stolen goods. Finally, these home visits have a service and referral function.

The Japanese police and social control apparatus is aided greatly by Crime Prevention Associations of local citizens in each district. These associations are especially valuable in the juvenile area. Wayward juveniles would soon feel the shame of their deviant behavior. Family, police, school, and neighborhood "good citizens" normally combine to keep potentially wayward youth in line (Clifford, 1976).

The social gain of this network of control agents is to produce conformity to existing standards. In so doing, however, there is the tendency to restrict innovative and rebellious behaviors that are socially desirable. The right to be different, to be left alone, falls victim to the number-one priority: the need to be part of the cohesive whole. It is a need that is seen as a supreme moral and social necessity in a land of great tradition, hoary rituals, and very limited resources. This social cohesion also produces "oversocialized" personalities (inner containment) and thus protects (insulates) the overseas Japanese from aberrant conduct, even to the second and third generations. The delinquency rates of overseas Japanese are characteristically the lowest of any other group except the Chinese (Reckless, 1961).

The Japanese themselves offer no coherent theoretical justification for the "low and decreasing crime rate" in Japan. The White Paper (1977) poses four reasons for this unique downward trend in the crime rate. First, the paper calls attention to the fact that "Japan may be considered as one centralized country with a single race and with common socio-economic and cultural backgrounds. This has saved Japan from crimes caused by racial issues such as economic insecurity, subordination, or incomplete participation" (p. 21). Second, postwar affluence, physical security, and high educational attainment of the population have combined to offer potential criminals legitimate opportunities for achievement and success. Third, informal institutional controls through the family, school, community, and factory historically have been successful in maintaining an orderly society and currently in "preventing and controlling crime problems." Fourth, the paper cites the highly efficient Japanese formal control system. Parenthetically, and somewhat apologetically, or so it seems, the White Paper credits Japan's very strict gun control laws for the low rates of armed robbery and homicide. "In Japan the inability to procure suitable firearms with which to commit such crimes strongly discourages persons prone to commit them."

In our current haste to "copy" anything Japanese—from making cars to stamping out lawbreaking—there is the danger that an indigenous and culturally integrated system of formal and informal controls will be transplanted into the infertile soil of the U.S. and Western European societies. It is our opinion that some specific techniques can be incorporated into our formal control apparatus, such as the development of catchment areas, police minicenters, foot patrols, and even the establishment of new kinds of indigenous neighborhood crime prevention groups to supersede the Chicago Area Project, Back of the Yards, and Mobilization for Youth programs. But these new programs are unlikely to fare much better than their predecessors, the countless other community-oriented exemplary programs sponsored by LEAA in the 1970s.

Increasingly chaotic, if not yet anomic, postindustrial countries can indeed gain much from the Japanese experience in crime prevention and control, especially if we are aware that crime prevention and control are but a reflection of a socially cohesive society. Without moving too far afield from the Crime Control and Due Process models, Japan is the only nation that has come from feudalism to modernity in five decades without experiencing the disorganization, culture conflict, and anomie currently being felt by the developing nations and historically felt by Western nations. It could have been otherwise.

Reischauer (1964) calls attention to some of the problems faced by Japan in achieving this rapid and unparalleled transformation. Chief among them are the stresses inherent in the changed age and sex roles, particularly the former. So great was the strain on traditional values that in the postwar period of the 1950s, the attraction of Marxist ideology for the young very nearly crumbled the "cake of custom" and with it centuries of unrelieved patriarchal and clan control in personal and political affairs. Additional inequalities and conflicts were those of differential socioeconomic status and major rural-urban conflicts. In short, Japan confronted the same problems in becoming a modern society that plague other countries.

A close reading of the extensive historical and cultural literature suggests that apart from the unusual circumstances that Japan alone faced in achieving modernization, three special elements played a role in its social and economic transformation to a modern state. First, the racial and cultural homogeneity of Japan was an unmatched advantage in making the transition. There were few "outsiders," and for hundreds of years Japan limited contacts with strangers and their ways. Thus, modernization presented a threat to *everyone* in the nation and the response was *total* rather than segmental. Unlike the West, it was not a question of integrating or melting newcomers. In Japan, everyone was a newcomer in the new industrial state. Hence, normative changes were at once easier and yet more difficult. The new rules had to conform to new functional necessities, say, to the assembly line and the factory system, and yet maintain continuity with the past.

Second, Japan's homogeneity of population and its isolation created an integrated and cohesive system unmatched anywhere in the West. In contrast to other traditional societies and even to China, the Japanese evolved a two-pronged system of control: familial and clan, *and* allegiance to a central authority (Levy, 1970). When familial control was put to the challenge by the achievement ethic and other concomitants of modernization, loyalty to the central authority remained. This legitimate authority was never threatened. In short, even in the premodern state, a centralized authority structure vital for the functioning of any modern society already existed. Though the more intimate levels of authority—family and neighborhood—were seriously threatened, the legitimacy of the central authority, whether shogunate or imperial, continued. When "normalcy" returned after the U.S. occupation, the primary institutions, especially the family, reasserted legitimate authority. The reassertion of primary controls, coupled with loyalty to the "state," is probably the reason for the significant and continuous decline observed in the Japanese crime rate in the postwar era.

Third, the "this worldness" of Japanese religious and cultural values did not force a choice on the Japanese of maintaining traditional standards or accepting the values inherent in modernization.

In short, the Japanese moved from one form of mechanical solidarity to another not very different form. And as Durkheim and other early sociologists knew, social cohesion facilitates social control and minimizes social deviance. The Japanese Social Control model of crime control is, therefore, not the cause but the result of a social and cultural organization that promotes civility and a very low rate of street crime.

## References

Bayley, D. 1976. *Public Behavior in Japan and in the U.S.* Berkeley: University of California Press.
Beccaria, C. 1804. *Essay on Crime and Punishment.* 415 ed. E. Newberry, London.
Bentham, J. 1830. *The Rationale of Punishment.* London: Robert Heward.
Clifford, W. 1976. *Crime Control in Japan.* Lexington, Mass.: Lexington Books.
de Tocqueville, A. 1945. *Democracy in America.* New York: Vintage Books.
Dinitz, S. 1981. *Preventing Crime and Juvenile Delinquency.* The Hague, The Netherlands: International Union of Local Authorities.
Levy, M.J., Jr. 1970. "Contrasting Factors in the Modernization of China and Japan." In *Comparative Perspectives: Theories and Methods*, edited by A. Etzioni and F.L. Dubow, pp. 225-67. Boston: Little, Brown.
Ministry of Justice Japan. 1977. Summary of the White Paper on Crime, Tokyo, Japan: Government of Japan.
Packer, H.L. 1969. *The Limits of the Criminal Sanction.* Stanford: Stanford University Press, pp. 167-68.
Reckless, W.C. 1961. "A New Theory of Delinquency and Crime." *Federal Probation* 25, no. 4: pp. 42-46.
Reischauer, M. 1964. *Japan Past and Present.* 3d. ed. New York: A.A. Knopf.
Shinnar, S., and K. Shinnar. 1975. "The Effect of the Criminal Justice System on the Control of Crime: A Quantitative Approach." *Law and Society Review* 9:581-61.
Van den Haag, E. 1975. *Punishing Criminals: Concerning a Very Old and Painful Question.* New York: Basic Books.
Vogel, E. 1979. *Japan as Number One.* New York: Harper.

# 8

# Theory, Pseudotheory, and Metatheory

*Joan McCord*

Theories about the causes of crime come in as many flavors as cheeses. Soft theories can be as elegant and interesting as a Belgium remoudou.[1] They tend to spread and to cling. Psychoanalytic theory and labeling theory come to mind. Fresh theories, like their counterparts in cream cheese or mitzithra, have done little ripening. Both biological theories (e.g. that XYY chromosomes cause crime) and psychological theories (e.g. that children need fathers or love) provide examples. They tie together bits of information that might otherwise appear as merely accidentally related. Semihard theories, like a fontina, have the advantage of versatility. Social learning theory and control theory illustrate the style. And finally, hard theories decorate research results, as does a parmesan, adding flavor as well as interest.

Theories about the causes of crime, in all varieties, have presupposed facts and relations among the facts. When those facts and relationships have been subjected to test, however, they have received but slight support.

Having already carried the cheese metaphor too far, I nevertheless use it to organize a discussion and demarcation of theories. Then I turn to metatheoretical issues, suggesting that adequate theories should meet criteria that include giving an account of "pretested facts."

## Hard Theories

"Hard" theories successfully describe the particular sets of events for which they have been designed. Some authors (e.g. Zetterberg, 1965) describe such theories as systems of verifiable propositions. Absent a clear specification of their range of application, theories of this type have the appearance of being universal.

Unfortunately, verifiable theories run into trouble from three sources. First, the concepts of confirmation, relevance, and evidence invite what Hempel (1965) calls "paradoxical instances," instances that conflict with clear criteria for the use of these concepts in social science. Most troublesome, perhaps, is the problem that a theory appears to be confirmed by instances for which the theory has no obvious application. The example used by Hempel, that "All ravens are black" is confirmed by every instance in which a nonblack thing is not a raven, serves as a paradigm. None of the many attempts to establish formal criteria for relevance have been successful in admitting only appropriate evidence.

Second, the choice involved in falsification depends, at least in part, upon "recalcitrant experience" (Quine, 1953). One can adjust the collection of one's beliefs to allow for any evidence; thus, no evidence need be accepted as demonstrating that a belief or a theory is false.

And third, the ways in which events are described determine which theories will be supported by the evidence (Goodman, 1955). An infinite number of descriptions can accurately describe any given set of events. Only some of the possible descriptions will be helpful in identifying causal relationships. For example, describing a forest fire as an "act of God" will affect whether the destruction is covered by insurance, but this description will not serve the forest rangers who hope to prevent future fires. Describing the same forest fire as beginning in a campground could help the forest rangers, but might be useless for a lumberman who wants to know the scope of his loss. Whether a description used in a given theory, describing one set of events, will be appropriate for another set of events must be an empirical question.

Consider, for example, the ecological theory proposed by Clifford Shaw and Henry McKay (1931). Shaw and McKay explained the distribution of crimes in relation to social mobility and social disorganization. As cities grow, they argued, successful people move away from densely populated areas that lack social organization. The densely populated areas continue to have high crime rates because they lack social organization.

The ecological theory has been justly criticized because it focuses only on street crimes. As Edwin Sutherland ([1949] 1983) noted, not all types of crimes are linked with inner-city sites. In addition, effects of ecological processes have changed through time (Bursik and Webb, 1982). Probably the most important criticism of the ecological theory, however, is that some street crimes thrive on social organization. Thus, although the Shaw and McKay theory fitted the facts on which it was developed, it does not correctly describe criminal activities at other times and places.

The mistake of fact has not been innocuous. Believing that social organization might decrease crime, designers of prevention programs have sought to increase a sense of community among juveniles living in high delin-quency areas. In *Street Gangs and Street Workers*, M.W. Klein (1971) re-ported the results of these efforts in Los Angeles. As expected, youth groups in the targeted areas lacked cohesiveness. Social workers participated in organizing activities; a reading program drew new members into the gang and increased cohesiveness. Crime increased. With each group, increased organization was associated with increased crime. Klein concluded: "Group-oriented gang intervention programs may serve to increase the very types of offenses of most concern to the public and to enforcement agencies" (p. 119).

Newer "hard" theories presuppose other facts to suggest causes of crime. The theory of differential association (Sutherland and Cressey, [1924] 1974), for example, postulates that criminals have been exposed to higher proportions of definitions of situations that are favorable to law violations. Strain theories (Cloward and Ohlin, 1960; Cohen, 1955; Kaplan, 1980; Merton, 1938) postulate that criminals have been frustrated in their at-tempts to achieve middle-class goals.

Although propositions in the theories resemble predictive scientific claims, perhaps it would be wiser to view these theories in a different way: as explanatory. Like explanations for other types of events, the success of these theories depends largely on their ability to satisfy curiosity. But what satisfies curiosity need not be testable. (Consider Aristotle's explanation of vertical movement: "A thing then which has the one kind of matter is light and always moves upward, while a thing which has the opposite matter is heavy and always moves downward," Bk. IV, Ch. 4.) Differential associa-tion theory and strain theories have been successful in presenting stories about the world that integrate the unusual with the usual, the strange with the familiar. These theories emphasize different points, paint different pic-tures.

In a provocative article on religion, John Wisdom ([1944] 1957) outlined a class of events for which adequate theory falls between mere opinions and scientific claims. Within this class of events, opposing theories depend upon taking a position. His examples include court decisions about whether a person has exercised reasonable care, a discussion about whether a couple has been happily married, and a debate about whether a scene is beautiful. Wisdom refers to the arguments favoring a particular theory of the type that presents a point of view as being "like the legs of a chair, not the links of a chain" (p. 157).

Differential association theory and strain theories describe the causes of crime in ways to suggest that criminal behavior belongs to the class of events that can best be explained by taking a point of view. Lawyers use such theories as they develop a case. Artists use such theories as they try different techniques for rendering a painting or text. And criminologists can legitimately use such theories when they attempt to present a perspective about criminal activities. Perhaps theories of this type should not be considered incomplete versions of falsifiable theories.

## Fresh Theories

One of the more enduring "fresh" theories about the causes of crime implicates broken homes. Widespread prevalence of broken homes among delinquents in New York (Slawson, 1923), London (Burt, 1925), Chicago (Shaw and McKay, 1932), Boston (Glueck and Glueck, 1950), Philadelphia (Monahan, 1957), and rural California (Merrill, 1947) seem to give credit to the theory. Despite the popular appeal of the theory, too little attention has been given alternative explanations to warrant a conclusion that broken homes cause crimes.

Daniel Glaser (1986) pointed out that the overrepresentation of broken homes among criminal populations is particularly pronounced for adjudicated crimes, and that adjudicated crimes reflect judges' beliefs that broken homes are inadequate. Thus, some of the evidence used to support a belief that broken homes cause crime seems to have been caused by that belief. Furthermore, youths who are adjudicated delinquents typically have prior histories of serious misbehavior (Black and Reiss, 1970; Erickson and Empey, 1963; Farrington, 1986; Short and Nye, 1958). If the onset of delinquency precedes parental absence, it would be misleading to attribute crime to parental absence.

A child's behavior appears to generate what Paterson (1986) calls a "coercive cycle." Such coercive cycles would be expected to increase tensions between the parents as well as between a parent and a child. To the extent that yelling and other aversive behaviors contribute to marital disruption, it would be reasonable to conclude that children's misbehavior causes broken homes. Could it be possible that instead of the divorce leading to a child's misbehavior, the child's misbehavior might actually cause the divorce? Support for this interpretation can be gathered from a study designed for other purposes. Mitchell, Cronkite, and Moos (1983) collected data from a sample of adult depressed, married patients, their spouses, and a community sample of husbands and wives randomly selected to match the patients in social class. As part of a measure of chronic stress, their data included a rating of children's emotional problems during the prior twelve months. A family support measure reflected mutual helpfulness, open expressions of favorable feelings, and absence of conflict. Among all four groups, the stress measure including children's prior problems correlated with the measure showing lack of current emotional support within the family.

Another possibility is that broken homes are associated with crime because of characteristics among parents (e.g. violence or alcoholism) that produce criminal behavior and also contribute to marital discord. In a longitudinal study of males, McCord (1982) found that a significantly larger proportion of boys raised in single-parent families had alcoholic fathers. The alcoholism, rather than paternal absence, appeared to account for serious crime. The same study showed that single-parent and intact families were equally likely to produce criminals if the mother was affectionate. Because the single-parent homes generated higher crime rates in the absence of maternal affection, it seemed reasonable to conclude that fathers in two-parent homes provide an alternate source of affection. A much lower proportion of the single-parent families provided supervision after school. Controlling for supervision, criminal rates among boys reared in broken homes and intact homes were almost identical. Rather than broken homes, lack of affection and of supervision appeared to be criminogenic.

In the absence of additional studies, other interpretations are certainly plausible. Perhaps, as McCord and Wadsworth (1985) suggest, societal expectations of troublesome behavior create high rates of crime among those raised in broken homes. Evidence showing that behavior is responsive to expectations can be found in studies as varied as the demonstrations of hypnotic response to suggestions (Barber and Calverley, 1964, 1965; Orne, 1959), emotional responses to injections of epinephrine (Schacter, 1964), judgments of tone as affected by a shill (Zobel and Lehman, 1969), and identification of pain thresholds as influenced by models (Craig and Theiss, 1971). Laboratory studies measuring evaluation of performance have shown that identical acts tend to be judged differently when attributed to men and to women (Pheterson et al., 1971). Bizarre episodes among patients in mental hospitals occur more frequently when staff are available to respond (Melbin, 1969). These studies seem to show effects of social expectations. Because of the widespread belief that broken homes are detrimental, children from broken homes may find their roles confirmed when they misbehave. If so, crime rates might be more effectively reduced by changing social expectations than by making divorce more difficult.

Other "fresh" theories, like the theory that broken homes lead to crime, have been viewed within too narrow a context. Evidence that genetic factors influence crime has sometimes been confused with evidence favoring particular theories about genetic loading. Ignorance about sequences of events and the influence of culture poses particular hazards to such theories.

Theories that criminals have failed to learn society's rules because they have slow autonomic recovery rates assume that autonomic nervous system responses cause learning differences. Learning differences could, however, be responsible for the measured autonomic responses.

That learning can influence autonomic responses has been demonstrated through teaching phobic women techniques for coping with spiders (Bandura et al., 1985). Catecholamine secretions responded to training and to the women's perceptions of their own coping abilities. After training, the researchers measured catecholamine reactivity with the women unable to control interaction with the spiders. Epinephrine and norepinephrine increased, a reaction inconsistent with deconditioning. The authors concluded: "Strengthening perceptions of coping efficacy to maximal level eliminated any differential catecholamine reactivity to the previously intimidating tasks" (p. 413).

Very early experiences could affect autonomic responses. To the extent that early development influences subsequent behavior, identification of proper sequencing becomes difficult. Even when measures are taken at different times, it will not always be possible to know whether that which has been measured first has ontological priority as well.

Among the events that could influence causal relations between slow autonomic responses and crime are punitive social experiences. Criminals may have learned to ignore pain. Laboratory experiments show that exposure to violence has a desensitizing effect (Cline et al., 1973; Thomas et al., 1977). Studies also have shown that criminals are more likely than noncriminals to have been exposed to physical abuse (Bandura and Walters, 1959; Farrington, 1978; Glueck and Glueck, 1950; McCord, 1983). Without evidence about early autonomic responsiveness, one cannot distinguish between differences introduced by socialization and biological differences affecting how infants respond to similar socialization practices.

Sequencing questions arise in attempting to decide which personality characteristics are inherited and which arise in response to socialization practice. Furthermore, studies carried out in similar cultures cannot disclose the contribution of culture to relationships.

## Soft Theories

"Soft" theories spread into criminology after attaining a degree of acceptance as explanations for noncriminal behavior. These theories are so nebulous that they continue to influence criminologists despite relatively clear examples showing that developments from their premises have failed to produce predicted results.

Psychoanalytic theories assume that "superego development," conscience, requires internalization of parental prohibitions. Boys come to control their instinctual desires, according to theory, by learning to inhibit libidinal attachments to their mothers. According to Freudian theory, criminal behavior represents poor psychosexual development (Fenichel, 1945; Freud, 1905; Meerloo, 1956). Whiting et al. (1958) attributed high crime rates in lower-class cultures to what they perceived as a matriarchal social milieu. Bacon et al. (1963) tested the theory by comparing crime rates among forty-eight nonliterate societies that had also been rated for the degree to which they provided opportunities "to identify with the father." The negative correlation between the crime scales and the father-identification scale supported the authors' conclusion that "lack of opportunity for the young boy to form a masculine identification is in itself an important antecedent of crime" (p. 299).

Psychoanalytic theories led to development of treatment facilities that attempted to retrain delinquents. These have been described in such books as *Wayward Youth* (Aichhorn, 1935), *Love Is Not Enough* (Bettelheim, 1950), and *Controls from Within* (Redl and Wineman, 1954). At best these and other attempts to mold personality using the psychoanalytic model have had modest success.

Labeling theories account for behavior by showing that it is a response to expectations (Kitsuse 1962; Lemert, 1951; Rosenthal, 1966). Examples of such responsiveness have been noted in the effects of marijuana (Becker, 1963) and aggressive responses to alcohol (Lang et al., 1975; Steele and Southwick, 1985). Because court adjudications involve assigning a role as delinquent, further criminal behavior could be a reaction to the criminal justice system label (Ageton and Elliott, 1974; Farrington and Bennett, 1981; Garfinkel, 1956).

Labeling theories resemble psychoanalytic theories in their appeal to complex internal "forces" that drive behavior. Whereas psychoanalytic theory postulated id, ego, and superego, labeling theories postulate a "self-concept" as the fundamental motivating force. Whereas psychoanalytic theory led to institutions that practiced milieu therapy, labeling theory contributed to deinstitutionalization and "diversion" of delinquents from the courts. Attempts to measure reductions in crime attributable to diversion, however, have yielded few encouraging signs (Elliott et al., 1978; Gibbons and Blake, 1976; Klein, 1974, 1979; McCord, 1985; Severy and Whitaker, 1982).

Both psychoanalytic and labeling theory tell interesting stories. Their proponents appear to be committed interpreters, seeking instances that demonstrate their theories. Edwin M. Schur (1971) wrote in defense of a labeling perspective: "Some specific forms of deviation may, it is true, lend themselves less readily to labeling analysis than do others. . . . borderline forms of deviance seem to be especially good candidates for labeling analysis and those deviations on which widespread consensus exists (homicide, incest, and so on) less promising candidates" (p. 21).

Although some evidence suggests that encounters with the criminal justice system increase crime (Farrington, 1977), it would be a mistake to conclude that such evidence confirms labeling theory. Alternative possibilities include effects of arrest on perceptions of justice. If encounters with the police increase the delinquent's sense of injustice or resentment, for example, criminality might be increased without a change in self-concept.

## Semihard Theories

Social learning theories (Akers, 1973; Bandura and Walters, 1963; Trasler, 1962) and control theories (Hirschi, 1969; Reckless and Dinitz, 1967, 1972) have been widely accepted in criminology. These account for criminality in terms of rewards, punishments, and models of behavior. Both theories assume universal psychological hedonism, though psychological hedonism has not received the critical examination that its place in these theories would seem to require.

At pains to defend morality as rational, Joseph Butler (1726) delivered a famous attack on psychological hedonism. (1) Any cogent description of human nature must account for the appearance of benevolence, of filial love, of a disposition to friendship. If genuine love were restricted to self-love, there could be no accounting for a preference to benefit particular others. (2) Happiness requires the satisfaction of specific desires. What is desired, say food or the well-being of another, could not be the happiness itself or we would not have those specific appetites the satisfaction of which (sometimes) produces happiness. (3) When we hear of actions by others we often make moral judgments about them even when there would be no possibility that we could be affected. (4) The method by which happiness is obtained ("gratification of certain affections, appetites, passion") has been confused with the objects that satisfy them. Some people receive pleasure from benefiting others or pursuing justice; some people receive pleasure from being praised or made wealthy. Both sets of appetites are attached to motivation in the same way: as the objects of desire.

To the above arguments, David Hume ([1777] 1960) added that (5) animals frequently show extreme kindness toward people as well as to other animals. It is implausible to attribute to them "refined deductions of self-interest." The sacrifice of parents for their children, expressions of gratitude, and the generosity of sentiment sometimes found between a man and woman appear to be disinterested benevolence. "These and a thousand other instances are marks of a general benevolence in human nature, where no *real* interest binds us to the object. And how an *imaginary* interest known and avowed for such, can be the origin of any passion or emotion, seems difficult to explain" (p. 143).

An "egotistic bias" has infected many types of psychological research. Lynn and Oldenquist (1986) show how restricting that bias has been in relation to finding solutions for problems that require both community action and personal sacrifice. Their examples include voter apathy, overpopulation, and pollution. They might also have included payment of taxes, compliance with contracts, and obedience to laws.

If self-interest is not the only motivator, rewards and punishments may be unnecessary for teaching children how to act. The use of these incentives may in fact encourage children to become self-centered. Children might be taught to respond to praise and blame, to musical signals, or simply to directions. Too little evidence about infant motivations is available for any reasonable conclusion regarding human nature.

A study of three-to-four-year-old children suggests, however, that neither reinforcement theory nor social deprivation theory does justice to children's willingness to comply with parents' requests (Parpal and Maccoby, 1985). Mothers of these children were randomly assigned to one of three groups. One group of mothers was shown how to imitate a child and to avoid giving directions. Those mothers were asked to practice the technique with their own children for one week. At the end of the week, the mothers and their children were brought to a mobile laboratory. The mother-child pairs of the group who had been trained were asked to play for fifteen minutes as they had been playing during the practice sessions. Mother-child pairs in the second group were asked to play as they normally do for fifteen minutes. The remaining mother-child pairs were told that the mother would be helping the experimenter by completing questionnaires during the fifteen minutes; the children were asked not to cross a line separating a playing space from the mothers' part of the room. After the fifteen minutes, mothers in all three groups gave specific directions (controlled through earphones) to their children. At this point the mothers were not allowed to coax or to praise their children. An observer blind to the conditions of the pairs scored the children for compliance. The experimenters reasoned that mothers naturally use subtle rewards for compliance; if rewards and punishments teach obedience, the free-play situation should generate the most compliance. In fact, this group showed the least compliance. Children whose mothers had spent the preliminary time answering a questionnaire and those whose mothers had been responsive to their requests were significantly more responsive to their mothers' requests. The authors suggest that the only thing the latter two groups had in common was the absence of attempts to control. Of course there are other descriptions as well: both groups of mothers whose children were about equally compliant, for example, were exhibiting a willingness to do as others asked.

## Metatheories and Alternatives

None of the theories discussed above has been notably successful in identifying which individuals would become criminals. Nor has any provided a clear foundation for successful prevention programs. Hoping to improve this record, many criminologists have combined older theories.

Glaser (1978, 1979), for example, melded differential association and control theory with opportunity theory to form a theory of differential anticipation. Greenwood and Zimring (1985) integrated control and social learning theories with physical theories and opportunity theory. Elliott and his colleagues (1979, 1985) combined strain, control, and social learning theories with a modified version of differential association theory. Klein and Mednick (1982) combined a form of learning theory (aversive inhibitory conditioning theory) with labeling theory, suggesting that biological differences determine whether criminal sanctions decrease criminality. Wilson and Herrnstein (1985) integrated a biological view of intelligence and preference with social learning theory to account for differences in proclivities toward crime. Farrington et al. (1986) constructed a theory that combines elements of strain theories, differential association theory, social learning theory, and control theory.

The new metatheories are likely to improve predictions, if for no other reason than that they involve more variables than simple theories do. As a trade-off, underlying conceptual confusions and false assumptions are likely to be more difficult to detect.

Analysis of a particular theory will bring the issue into focus. Mednick and his coworkers (Pollock et al., 1983) studied Danish records on several thousand adopted men whose biological and sociological fathers' criminal convictions were known. Criminal records were found among 15 percent of those whose biological parents were not criminals but whose adoptive parents included a criminal, and among 20 percent of those whose adoptive parents were not criminals but whose biological parents included a criminal. The difference suggests that biogenetic factors have a part in the production of crime.

Mednick and Volavka (1980) proposed an explanation: criminals inherit neurological systems that impede reduction of fear and therefore interfere with learning. In support of this "biosocial theory," its proponents point to the relatively low levels of skin conductance and the slow latency of response found among criminals in several studies.

Evidence on at least four issues ought to be sought before Mednick's biosocial theory becomes an accepted explanation. First, the heritability of physiological response differences should be checked. Slow response rates could be typical of criminals and yet not be the inherited condition to which the adoption studies point. Evidence has not yet shown that adopted sons of criminals have low levels of skin conductance or slow latency of response. The slow response rates found among (nonadopted) criminals could reflect differences in experience related to criminality, but not be inherited characteristics.

Second, the primary assumption that learning how to act requires fear needs confirmation. On its face this assumption appears to be either circular or false. Children often seem to do what they are asked without any sign of a potential sanction. Of course, one can imagine any number of possible rewards or punishments that could be motivational, but imagined confirmation should not be accepted as evidence. In short, the underlying assumption of psychological hedonism has not been demonstrated.

Third, more work should be done to test the relationship between the measured autonomic system responses and the attributed emotions. Whether skin conductance indicates dissipation of fear or whether slow recovery rates represent hyporesponsiveness has been questioned by several researchers (e.g. Blackburn, 1978; Hare, 1978; Mawson and Mawson, 1977; Siddle and Trasler, 1981).

Fourth, the temporal order between slow autonomic responses and punitive social experiences among criminals needs study. As mentioned above, studies have shown that exposure to pain tends to desensitize. Such exposure could account for the slight effect that punishments appear to have when administered to criminals.

A more fruitful approach, in my opinion, has been begun by David Farrington, Lloyd Ohlin, and James Q. Wilson (1986). They have sketched questions that theories ought to address, among them, Why do criminals continue criminal activities? Why is there versatility rather than specialization? Why does crime peak at ages 15 to 18? Why does the probability of recidivism increase with each successive offense? Why are family child-rearing techniques the best predictors of onset? Whether these or a different set of questions should be set forth, it seems clear that criminology would advance more rapidly were there a list of critical facts about which an adequate theory of crime causation must give an account.

A theory of arithmetic, for example, must allow for certitude, an infinite supply of numbers, transitivity, identity, and an inverse. Any theory that cannot account for all of these would not be considered a theory of arithmetic. The set theoretical approach to arithmetic of Frege ([1884] 1950) and the type theoretical approach of Russell ([1903] 1937) differ for other reasons. A theory of ethics must account for feelings of guilt, moral dilemmas, the motivational force of moral judgments, and the possibility that we can know the better and do the worse. Externalists (e.g. Kant, [1785] 1959; Moore, [1903] 1959) and internalists (Hume, [1777] 1960; Plato, 1956) give different accounts of these phenomena. A theory of language must account for an infinite supply of sentences composed of a finite vocabulary, the possibility for children to learn the language, and a distinction between use and meaning. A theory of combustion must account for an increase in weight and release of energy. A theory of light must account for rectilinear propagation, reflection, refraction, scattering, and absorption. For what must a criminal theory give an account?

Psychosocial theories, like biosocial theories, are subject to errors of mistaken sequencing. Social learning theory asserts that people repeat behavior that is rewarded and avoid behavior that is punished. Maccoby (1980) summarized: "Children learn from their own experience with pleasant or painful outcomes and also by example" (p. 336).

Studies of family socialization practices have seemed to present a coherent picture of the development of antisocial behavior. Rejection, harsh or inconsistent discipline, and parental conflict mark the homes of criminals more frequently than those of noncriminals (Farrington and West, 1981; McCord, 1979, 1982; Olweus, 1980; Pulkkinen, 1983). These descriptions seem to depict parents who do not reinforce good behavior and who model successful aggressive behavior. Several studies measured parental behavior before the occurrence of delinquency, so their evidence has been interpreted as demonstrating that parental behavior caused criminal behavior. Yet, misbehavior predicts further misbehavior (Farrington, 1979, 1986; McCord, 1980, 1985; Mitchell and Rosa, 1981; Robins, 1978). And the earlier misbehavior may have elicited the erratic, rejecting, harsh parental behavior.

Children may generate different forms of socialization. That adults prefer children who smile, talk spontaneously with adults, and look them in the eye has been demonstrated in the laboratory (Cantor and Gelfand, 1977). As Wilson and Herrnstein (1985) suggest, children may differentially inherit the qualities leading parents to enjoy holding them, feeding them, and otherwise socializing them in ways that produce prosocial behavior.

According to social learning theory, socialization typically involves using approval as a reward and disapproval or physical pain as punishment. Yet, people voluntarily and frequently risk pain. For example, they play contact sports. Clearly, too, people often place themselves outside the range of potential approval.

Theories invoking a striving for status, a desire for success, and a search for enhanced self-esteem seem to provide explanations of why delinquents do poorly in school (e.g. Cloward and Ohlin, 1960; Glaser, 1978; Kaplan,

1980). Yet, many programs designed to increase success in school have failed to prevent delinquency (Gersten et al., 1979; Jones et al., 1981). We need more evidence about the links between school success and delinquency.

Laboratory studies have shown that unexpectedly good results can be more disturbing to the recipients than expectedly mediocre results (Austin and Walster, 1974), and laboratory studies have shown that rewards sometimes create disincentives (Greene and Lepper, 1974; Lepper and Greene, 1978; Schwartz, 1982). Such studies raise the possibility that success in school may be disturbing to some youngsters and that school failure need not be frustrating.

The opponent-process theory (Solomon, 1980) suggests conditions under which punishment and reward operate in opposition to what has been considered their typical reinforcement valences. If Solomon is correct, criminals may have acquired a taste for the pains administered in attempts to deter their activities.

We need to know how people learn to view particular things as rewards and other things as punishments. Very possibly, using something as a reward is one way of teaching what to count as a pleasure. Using something as a punishment may teach people *to be* pained by that thing. At a minimum the direction of learning is unclear. In view of an obvious diversity in the sorts of events that operate as incentives, predictions must be incomplete without knowledge of who will find what an incentive.

Both differential association theory and labeling theory focus on the interface between social phenomena and individual perceptions. According to differential association theory, people learn how to act through exposure to definitions of situations, becoming delinquent in response to an excess of definitions favorable to violations of the law. According to labeling theory, people act in response to the role expectations they encounter. Both theories suggest that behavior follows from social milieu. Neither adequately addresses questions about differential selection of friends, of spouses, and of significant others.

Criminologists have a wide range of theories from which to choose. In discussing this range, I have argued that theories can serve more than one legitimate purpose. Also, as metatheory, I have tried to show that the practice of legitimizing theories requires careful attention to assumptions as well as to derivations.

Criminology should be aimed at understanding crime as well as at its control. We have, it seems to me, paid too little attention to the requirements of legitimacy for theories not cast in the mold of logical positivism. Providing a reasonable story, having a reasonable theory in this sense, should require establishing that events occur in the sequences implied by the theory. If the theory includes putative motives, legitimation requires evidence that those motives have in fact been operative.

For theories that aim at prevention of crime, legitimacy requires attention to the hazards of misspecification. Misidentification of the descriptions under which one event is causally related to another can result in grave errors of estimation.

Criminology needs more than a multiflavored approach to theories. We need to identify critical events against which to measure the adequacy of theories. We need, in particular, to learn more about the sequence of events leading to criminal behavior. And we need to learn more about motivation—about motivation in general as well as about motivation that leads to crimes.

## Notes

1. The author wishes to thank Daniel Glaser, Ann Witte, Carl Silver, Gwynne Netteler, and Rob McCord for their careful readings and helpful suggestions.

## References

Ageton, S., and D.S. Elliott. 1974. "The Effects of Legal Processing on Delinquent Orientations." *Social Problems* 22: 87-100.

Aichhorn, A. 1935. *Wayward Youth*. New York: Viking.

Akers, R.L. 1973. *Deviant Behavior: A Social Learning Approach*. Belmont, Calif.: Wadsworth.

Aristotle. *De Caelo* (335 B.C.) 1941 (Translated by J.L. Stocks). In *The Basic Works of Aristotle*, edited by R. McKeon. New York: Random House.

Austin, W., and E. Walster. 1974. "Reactions to Confirmations and Disconfirmations of Expectancies of Equity and Inequity." *Journal of Personality and Social Psychology* 30: 208-16.

Bacon, M.K., I.L. Child, and H. Barry, Jr. 1963. "A Cross-cultural Study of Correlates of Crime." *Journal of Abnormal and Social Psychology* 66: 291-300.

Bandura, A., C.B. Taylor, S.L. Williams, I.N. Mefford, and J.D. Barchas. 1985. "Catecholamine Secretion as a Function of Perceived Coping Self-efficacy." *Journal of Consulting and Clinical Psychology* 53: 406-14.

Bandura, A., and R.H. Walters. 1959. *Adolescent Aggression*. New York: Ronald Press.

_____. 1963. *Social Learning and Personality Development*. New York: Holt, Rinehart & Winston.

Barber, T.X., and D.S. Calverley. 1964. "Effects of E's Tone of Voice on 'Hypnoticlike' Suggestibility." *Psychological Reports* 15: 139-44.

_____. 1965. "Empirical Evidence for a Theory of Hypnotic Behavior: Effects on Suggestibility of Five Variables Typically Included in Hypnotic Induction Procedures." *Journal of Consulting Psychology* 29: 98-107.

Becker, H.S. 1963. *Outsiders*. Glencoe, Ill.: Free Press.

Bettelheim, B. 1950. *Love Is Not Enough*. Glencoe, Ill.: Free Press.

Black, D.J., and A.J. Reiss, Jr. 1970. "Police Control of Juveniles." *American Sociological Review* 34: 63-77.

Blackburn, R. 1978. "Psychopathy, Arousal, and the Need for Stimulation." In *Psychopathic Behavior*, edited by R.D. Hare and D. Schalling. Chichester: Wiley.

Bursik, R.J., Jr., and J. Webb. 1982. "Community Change and Patterns of Delinquency." *American Journal of Sociology* 88: 24-42.

Burt, C. 1925. *The Young Delinquent*. New York: Appleton.

Butler, Joseph. 1726. *Fifteen Sermons (including "Three Sermons Upon Human Nature")*. London.

Cantor, N.L., and D.M. Gelfand. 1977. "Effects of Responsiveness and Sex of Children on Adults' Behavior." *Child Development* 48: 232-38.

Cline, V.B., R.G. Croft, and S. Courrier. 1973. "Desensitization of Children to Television Violence." *Journal of Personality and Social Psychology* 27: 360-65.

Cloward, R.A., and L.E. Ohlin. 1960. *Delinquency and Opportunity*. New York: Free Press.

Cohen, A.K. 1955. *Delinquent Boys*. Glencoe, Ill.: Free Press.

Craig, L.D., and S.M. Theiss. 1971. "Vicarious Influences on Pain-threshold Determinations." *Journal of Personality and Social Psychology* 19: 53-59.

Elliott, D.S., S.S. Ageton, and R.J. Canter. 1979. "An Integrated Theoretical Perspective on Delinquent Behavior." *Journal of Research in Crime and Delinquency* 16: 3-27.

Elliott, D.S., F.W. Dunford, and B.A. Knowles. 1978. "Diversion—A Study of Alternative Processing Practices: An Overview of Initial Study Findings." Boulder, Colo.: Behavioral Research Institute.

Elliott, D.S., D. Huizinga, and S.S. Ageton. 1985. *Explaining Delinquency and Drug Use*. Beverly Hills: Sage.

Erickson, M.L., and L.T. Empey. 1963. "Court Records, Undetected Delinquency, and Decision-making." *Journal of Criminal Law, Criminology and Police Science* 54: 456-69.

Farrington, D.P. 1977. "The Effects of Public Labelling." *British Journal of Criminology* 17: 112-25.

———. 1978. "The Family Backgrounds of Aggressive Youths." In *Aggression and Antisocial Behaviour in Childhood and Adolescence*, edited by L.A. Hersov and M. Berger. Oxford: Pergamon Press.

———. 1979. "Environmental Stress, Delinquent Behavior, and Convictions." In *Stress and Anxiety*, vol. 6, edited by I.G. Sarason and C.D. Spielberger. New York: Wiley.

———. 1986. "Stepping Stones to Adult Criminal Careers." In *Development of Antisocial and Prosocial Behavior*, edited by D. Olweus, J. Block, and M.R. Yarrow. New York: Academic Press.

Farrington, D.P., and T. Bennett. 1981. "Police Cautioning of Juveniles in London." *British Journal of Criminology* 21: 123-35.

Farrington, D.P., L.E. Ohlin, and J.Q. Wilson. 1986. *Understanding and Controlling Crime*. New York: Springer-Verlag.

Farrington, D.P., and D.J. West. 1981. "The Cambridge Study in Delinquent Development" (United Kingdom). In *Prospective Longitudinal Research: An Empirical Basis for Primary Prevention*, edited by S.A. Mednick and A.E. Baert. Oxford: Oxford University Press.

Fenichel, O. 1945. *The Psychoanalytic Theory of Neurosis*. New York: Norton.

Frege, G. (1884) 1950. *Foundations of Arithmetic.* Translated by J.L. Austin. Oxford: Basil Blackwell.

Freud, S. 1905. *Three Essays on Sexuality.* London: Hogarth.

Garfinkel, H. 1956. "Conditions of Successful Degradation Ceremonies." *American Journal of Sociology* 61: 420-24.

Gersten, J.C., T.S. Langner, and O. Simcha-Fagan. 1979. "Developmental Patterns of Types of Behavioral Disturbance and Secondary Prevention." *International Journal of Mental Health* 7: 132-49.

Gibbons, D.C., and G.F. Blake. 1976. "Evaluating the Impact of Juvenile Diversion Programs." *Crime and Delinquency* 11: 411-20.

Glaser, D. 1978. *Crime in Our Changing Society.* New York: Holt, Rinehart & Winston.

_____. 1979. "A Review of Crime-causation Theory and Its Application." In *Crime and Justice*, vol.1, edited by N. Morris and M. Tonry, pp. 203-37. Chicago: University of Chicago Press.

_____. 1986. Personal communication, August 20.

Glueck, S., and E.T. Glueck. 1950. *Unraveling Juvenile Delinquency.* New York: Commonwealth Fund.

Goodman, N. 1955. *Fact, Fiction, and Forecast.* Cambridge: Harvard University Press.

Greene, D., and M.R. Lepper. 1974. "Effects of Extrinsic Rewards on Children's Subsequent Intrinsic Interest." *Child Development* 45: 1141-45.

Greenwood, P.W., and F.E. Zimring. 1985. *One More Chance.* Santa Monica, Calif.: Rand.

Hare, R.D. 1978. "Electrodermal and Cardiovascular Correlates of Psychopathy." In *Psychopathic Behaviour*, edited by R.D. Hare and D. Schalling. Chichester: Wiley.

Hempel, C.G. 1965. *Aspects of Scientific Explanation and Other Essays in the Philosophy of Science.* New York: Free Press.

Hirschi, T. 1969. *Causes of Delinquency.* Berkeley: University of California Press.

Hume, D. (1777) 1960. *An Enquiry Concerning the Principles of Morals.* La Salle, Ill.: Open Court.

Jones, R.R., M.R. Weinrott, and J.R. Howard. 1981. "Final Report: National Evaluation of the Teaching Family Model." Eugene, Ore.: Evaluation Research Group.

Kant, I. (1785) 1959. *Foundations of the Metaphysics of Morals.* Indianapolis: Bobbs-Merrill.

Kaplan, H.B. 1980. *Deviant Behavior in Defense of Self.* New York: Academic Press.

Kitsuse, J.I. 1962. "Societal Reaction to Deviant Behavior." *Social Problems* 9: 247-56.

Klein, M.W. 1971. *Street Gangs and Street Workers.* Englewood Cliffs, N.J.: Prentice-Hall.

_____. 1974. "Labelling, Deterrence and Recidivism: A Study of Police Dispositions of Juvenile Offenders." *Social Problems* 11: 292-303.

_____. 1979. "Deinstitutionalization and Diversion of Juvenile Offenders: A Litany of Impediments." In *Crime and Justice*, vol.1, edited by N. Morris and M. Tonry. Chicago: University of Chicago Press.

Klein, M.W., and S.A. Mednick. 1982. "Sanction Sensitivity: A Theory of Specific Deterrence of Delinquency." Paper presented at the Annual Meetings of the American Society of Criminology, Toronto.

Lang, A.R., D.J. Goeckner, V.J. Adesso, and G.A. Marlatt. 1975. "Effects of Alcohol on Aggression in Male Social Drinkers." *Journal of Abnormal Psychology* 84: 508-18.

Lemert, E. 1951. *Social Pathology.* New York: McGraw-Hill.

Lepper, M.R., and D. Greene. 1978. *The Hidden Costs of Reward.* Hillsdale, N.J.: Lawrence Erlbaum.

Lynn, M., and A. Oldenquist. 1986. "Egoistic and Nonegoistic Motives in Social Dilemmas." *American Psychologist* 41: 529-34.

Maccoby, E.E. 1980. *Social Development.* New York: Harcourt Brace Jovanovich.

Mawson, A.R., and C.D. Mawson. 1977. "Psychopathy and Arousal: A New Interpretation of the Psychophysiological Literature." *Biological Psychiatry* 12: 49-74.

McCord, J. 1979. "Some Child-rearing Antecedents of Criminal Behavior in Adult Men." *Journal of Personality and Social Psychology* 37: 1477-86.

———. 1980. "Patterns of Deviance." In *Human Functioning in Longitudinal Perspective: Studies of Normal and Psychopathological Populations,* edited by S.B. Sells, R. Crandall, M. Roff, J. Strauss, and W. Pollin. Baltimore: Williams & Wilkins.

———. 1982. "A Longitudinal View of the Relationship Between Paternal Absence and Crime." In *Abnormal Offenders, Delinquency, and the Criminal Justice System,* edited by J. Gunn and D.P. Farrington. Chichester: Wiley.

———. 1983. "A Forty Year Perspective on Effects of Child Abuse and Neglect." *Child Abuse and Neglect* 7: 265-70.

———. 1985. "Deterrence and the Light Touch of the Law." In *Reactions to Crime: The Public, the Police, Courts, and Prisons,* edited by D.P. Farrington and J. Gunn. London: Wiley.

McCord, J., and M.E.J. Wadsworth. 1985. "The Importance of Time in Stress and Stigma Paradigms." In *Stress and Stigma: Explanation and Evidence in the Sociology of Crime and Illness,* edited by U.E. Gerhardt and M.E.J. Wadsworth. New York: St. Martin's Press.

Mednick, S.A., and J. Volavka. 1980. "Biology and Crime." In *Crime and Justice,* vol. 2, edited by N. Morris and M. Tonry. Chicago: University of Chicago Press.

Meerloo, J.A.M. 1956. "The Father Cuts the Cord: The Role of the Father as Initial Transference Figure." *American Journal of Psychotherapy* 10: 472-80.

Melbin, M. 1969. "Behavior Rhythms in Mental Hospitals." *American Journal of Sociology* 74: 651-65.

Merrill, M.A. 1947. *Problems of Child Delinquency.* Boston: Houghton Mifflin.

Merton, R.K. 1938. "Social Structure and Anomie." *American Sociological Review* 3: 672-82.

Mitchell, R.E., R.C. Cronkite, and R.H. Moos. 1983. "Stress, Coping, and Depression among Married Couples." *Journal of Abnormal Psychology* 91: 433-48.

Mitchell, S., and P. Rosa. 1981. "Boyhood Behaviour Problems as Precursors of Criminality: A Fifteen-year Follow-up Study." *Journal of Child Psychology and Psychiatry* 11: 19-33.

Monahan, T. 1957. "Family Status and the Delinquent Child: A Reappraisal and Some New Findings." *Social Forces* 35: 251-58.

Moore, G.E. (1903) 1959. *Principia Ethica.* Cambridge: Cambridge University Press.

Olweus, D. 1980. "Familial and Temperamental Determinants of Aggressive Behavior in Adolescent Boys: A Causal Analysis." *Developmental Psychology* 16: 644-60.

144    Advances in Criminological Theory

Orne, M.T. 1959. "The Nature of Hypnosis: Artifact and Essence." *Journal of Abnormal and Social Psychology* 58: 277-99.
Parpal, M., and E.E. Maccoby. 1985. "Maternal Responsiveness and Subsequent Child Compliance." *Child Development* 56: 1326-44.
Patterson, G.R. 1986. "The Contribution of Siblings to Training for Fighting: A Microsocial Analysis." In *Development of Antisocial and Prosocial Behavior*, edited by D. Olweus, J. Block, and M.R. Yarrow. New York: Academic Press.
Pheterson, G., S.B. Kiesler, and P.A. Goldberg. 1971. "Evaluation of the Performance of Women as a Function of Their Sex, Achievement, and Personal History." *Journal of Personality and Social Psychology* 19: 114-18.
Plato, *Protagoras*. 1956. Translated by B. Jowett; revised by Martin Ostwald 1956. Indianapolis: Bobbs-Merrill.
Pollock, V., S.A. Mednick, and W.F. Gabrielli. 1983. "Crime Causation: Biological Theories." In *Encyclopedia of Crime and Justice*, vol. 1, edited by S.H. Kadish. New York: Free Press.
Pulkkinen, L. 1983. "Search for Alternatives to Aggression in Finland." In *Aggression in Global Perspective*, edited by A.P. Goldstein and M. Segall. Elmsford, N.Y.: Pergamon Press.
Quine, W.V.O. 1953. *From a Logical Point of View*. Cambridge: Harvard University Press.
Reckless, W.C., and S. Dinitz. 1967. "Pioneering with Self-Concept as a Vulnerability Factor in Delinquency." *Journal of Criminal Law, Criminology and Police Science* 58: 515-23.
———. 1972. *The Prevention of Juvenile Delinquency: An Experiment*. Columbus: Ohio State University.
Redl, F., and D. Wineman. 1954. *Controls From Within*. Glencoe, Ill.: Free Press.
Robins, L.N. 1978. "Aetiological Implications in Studies of Childhood Histories Relating to Antisocial Personality." In *Psychopathic Behaviour*, edited by R.D. Hare and D. Schalling. Chichester: Wiley.
Rosenthal, R. 1966. *Experimenter Effects in Behavioral Research*. New York: Appleton-Century-Crofts.
Russell, B. (1903) 1937. *The Principles of Mathematics*. London: Allen & Unwin; New York: Norton.
Schachter, S. 1964. "The Interaction of Cognitive and Physiological Determinants of Emotional State." In *Advances in Experimental Social Psychology*, edited by L. Berkowitz. New York: Academic Press.
Schur, E.M. 1971. *Labelling Deviant Behavior: Its Sociological Implications*. New York: Harper & Row.
Schwartz, B. 1982. "Reinforcement-induced Behavioral Stereotypy: How Not to Teach People to Discover Rules." *Journal of Experimental Psychology* 111: 23-39.
Severy, L., and J.M. Whitaker. 1982. "Juvenile Diversion: An Experimental Analysis of Effectiveness." *Evaluation Review* 6: 753-74.
Shaw, C., and H.D. McKay. 1931. *Social Factors in Juvenile Delinquency: A Study of the Community, the Family and the Gang in Relation to Delinquent Behavior*. Vol. 2 of *Report on the Causes of Crime*. Washington, D.C.: National Commission on Law Observance and Enforcement.
———. 1932. "Are Broken Homes a Causative Factor in Juvenile Delinquency?" *Social Forces* 10: 514-24.
Short, J.F., and F.I. Nye. 1958. "Extent of Unrecorded Juvenile Delinquency: Tenta-

tive Conclusions." *Journal of Criminal Law, Criminology and Police Science* 49: 296-302.

Siddle, D.A.T., and G.B. Trasler. 1981. "The Psychophysiology of Psychopathic Behaviour." In *Foundations of Psychosomatics*, edited by M.J. Christie and P.G. Mellett. Chichester: Wiley.

Slawson, J. 1923. "Marital Relations of Parents and Juvenile Delinquency." *Journal of Delinquency* 8: 280-83.

Solomon, R.L. 1980. "The Opponent-process Theory of Acquired Motivation: The Costs of Pleasure and the Benefits of Pain." *American Psychologist* 35: 691-712.

Steele, C.M., and L. Southwick. 1985. "Alcohol and Social Behavior: The Psychology of Drunken Excess." *Journal of Personality and Social Psychology* 48: 18-34.

Sutherland, E.H. (1949) 1983. *White Collar Crime*. New Haven: Yale University Press.

Sutherland, E.H., and D.R. Cressey. (1924) 1974. *Criminology*. 9th ed. Philadelphia: Lippincott.

Thomas, M.H., R.W. Horton, E.C. Lippincott, and R.S. Drabman. 1977. "Desensitization to Portrayals of Real-life Aggression as a Function of Exposure to Television Violence." *Journal of Personality and Social Psychology* 35: 450-58.

Trasler, G. 1962. *The Explanation of Criminality*. London: Routledge & Kegan Paul.

Whiting, J.W.M., R. Kluckhohn, and A. Anthony. 1958. "The Function of Male Initiation Ceremonies at Puberty." In *Readings in Social Psychology*, edited by E.E. Maccoby, T.M. Newcomb, and E.L. Hartley. New York: Holt, Rinehart & Winston.

Wilson, J.Q., and R.J. Herrnstein. 1985. *Crime and Human Nature*. New York: Simon & Schuster.

Wisdom, J. (1944) 1957. "Gods." Republished in *Philosophy and Psychoanalysis*. Oxford: Basil Blackwell.

Zetterberg, H.L. 1965. *On Theory and Verification in Sociology*. Totowa, N.J.: Bedminster Press.

Zoble, E.J., and R.S. Lehman. 1969. "Interaction of Subject and Experimenter Expectancy Effects in a Tone Length Discrimination Task." *Behavioral Science* 14: 357-63.

# Name Index

Adesso, V.J., 133. *See also* Goeckner, D.J., Lang Å. R., and Marlatt, G.A.

Ageton, Suzanne, 65, 133, 136. *See also* Elliott, Delbert and Huizinga, David

Aichhorn, A., 133

Akers, R.L. 81, 134. *See also* Burgess, R.L.

Aktar, S.N., 102. *See also* Singh, U.P.

Alexander, Yonah, 21. *See also* Freedman, Lawrence Z.

Allsop, J.F., 93. *See also* Feldman, M.P.

Amelang, M., 101. *See also* Rodel, G.

American Sociological Association, 80, 81

Andreason, N.C., 76

Anthony, A., 133. *See also* Kluckhorn, R. and Whiting, J.W.M.

Associated Press (reports quoted), 35

Austin, W., 139. *See also* Walster, E.

Bacon, M.K., 133. *See also* Child, I.L. and Barry, H., Jr.

Bandura, A., 134. *See also* Walters, R.H. and Taylor, C.B. 139

Barber, T.X., 131. *See also* Calverly, D.S.

Barratt, P., 90. *See also* Eysenck, H.J.

Barry, H., Jr., 133. *See also* Child, I.L. and Bacon, M.K.

Bayley, David, 122, 123

Beccaria, Cesare, 123

Becker, Herbert S., 133

Belson, W., 99

Bentham, Jeremy, 123

Berman, T., 100. *See also* Paisey, T.

Bernard, Thomas A., 17. *See also* Vold, George B.

Bettelheim, Bruno, 133

Black, Donald J., 130. *See also* Reiss, Albert J., Jr.

Blackburn, R., 137

Blake, G.F., 133. *See also* Gibbons, Don C.

Bloom, F.E., 74. *See also* Lazerson, A. and Hofstadter, L.

Bower, G.H., 77, 78. *See also* Hilgard, H.L.

Braithwaite, John, 40

Bridgman, P.W., 12

Burgess, P.K., 97, 101

Burgess, R.L., 81. *See also* Akers, R.L.

Burkhard, B., 77, 78. *See also* Domjan, M.

Bursik, R.J., Jr., 128. *See also* Webb, J.

Burt, C., 102, 130

Buss, Arnold, 60. *See also* Plomin, Robert

Butler, Joseph, 134

Calverley, D.S., 131. *See also* Barber, T.X.

Canter, R.J., 136. *See also* Ageton, Suzanne and Elliott, D.S.

Cantor, N.L., 138. *See also* Gelfand, D.M.

Carlson, N.E., 74, 77, 78

Carlton, P.L., 76

Carpenter, G.R., 80, 82. *See also* Gove, W.R.

Chapman, B., 104, 105, 106. *See also* Sinclair, I.

Child, I.L., 133. *See also* Bacon, M.K. and Barry, H., Jr.

Chrision, R.D., 94. *See also* Rushton, J.P.

Christiansen, K., 60. *See also* Mednick, Sarnoff

Clemente, A., 95. *See also* Silva, F. and Martorell, C.

Clemons, Samuel Langhorne, 1-16

Clifford, W., 113, 124

Clinard, Marshall B.; with Peter Yeager, 32, 33, 40, 41, 43, 45, 48; with Richard Quinney, 32, 39

Cline, V.B., 132. *See also* Croft, R.G. and Courrier, S.

Cloward, 80, 129, 138. *See also* Ohlin, Lloyd

Cohen, Albert K., 61, 80, 129

Cohen, Lawrence E., 62. *See also* Felson, Marcus

Cosa Nostra, 33. *See also* La Cosa Nostra

Coser, Lewis, 79, 81

Cote, G., 101. *See also* Leblanc, M.

147

# Subject Index